Belief in Ourselves

BELIEF IN OURSELVES

Neil M. Gunn

compiled by
Alistair McCleery and Dairmid Gunn

Whittles Publishing

Published by
Whittles Publishing Ltd.,
Dunbeath,
Caithness, KW6 6EG,
Scotland, UK

www.whittlespublishing.com

Introduction and Afterword © 2010 Dairmid Gunn and Alistair McCleery

ISBN 978-184995-022-0

Printed and bound in Scotland • www.airdrieprint.co.uk

Contents

Introduction

Neil M Gunn (1891 – 1973), one of Scotland's most distinguished and highly regarded novelists of the 20th century, was a prolific writer. While he is best known for his fictional work Gunn was also a perceptive and meditative essayist and he wrote extensively, throughout his life, on a wide range of subjects from landscape, nature and fishing to politics, nationalism and current affairs. An earlier collection of essays in a sister book, *Landscape to Light*, concentrates on his native landscape and culture and the spiritual aspects of his life and thought. This collection, *Belief in Ourselves*, focuses on politics in the widest sense, embracing group activity in all its forms from nationalism to both communal work in a social sense and co-operation in crofting and fishing; the focus extends also to literature as a source of inspiration for a nation and a provider of national identity. That most of the essays were written between the two world wars – a period of political uncertainty and economic crisis – brings a sense of urgency to the writer in terms of the resolution of the problems and the exploration of the ideas aired by him. Many of the problems he identifies remain with us, albeit in different forms. Indeed, the imaginative and enlightened way in which Gunn looks at the events of his day have a strange relevance for today's world. The essays are not in chronological order but are grouped according to subject. As with *Landscape to Light*, much of what Gunn writes informs his fictional work.

Neil Gunn, the son of a successful fishing boat skipper, was born in the small coastal village of Dunbeath in Scotland's most northerly county, Caithness, in which fishing and crofting were the principal means of livelihood. After an idyllic childhood in a landscape of moor, river and sea, Gunn was sent to pursue his secondary education at the hands of a tutor engaged by an elder sister married to a doctor in the south western county of Kirkcudbrightshire. From this tutor he received a sound grounding in English literature and a sufficient grasp of mathematics to pass the entrance examination for the Civil Service in 1907. Four years later he began his career in the Customs and Excise Service, which was to take him back to the Highlands where during the First World War he combined his customs and excise duties as a substitute officer with War work for the Admiralty. It was during these years that he developed a life-long friendship with the Irish novelist to be, Maurice Walsh, who was also a customs and excise officer. In 1921 he married a Highland girl from Dingwall, the county town of Ross and Cromarty, and two years later returned to the North. He was shocked to find Caithness in serious economic and social decline; fishing and crofting were particularly affected by the national economic crisis and evidence of this was to be seen in badly surfaced roads, inadequate fencing and silted up harbours. All this acted as stimulus for Gunn to indulge his creative instincts by writing. He had already written many articles and short stories, but not a novel. That was to come in 1926 when he was comfortably settled in Inverness on duties connected with the local Glen Mohr distillery. *The Grey Coast* (1926) and its successor, *The Lost Glen* (1932) were books in the realist mode, which reflected Gunn's bitterness and pessimism at that time. Neither book enjoyed much success. That had to await the appearance of a book written after *The Lost Glen*, but published before it, *Morning Tide* (1931). A Book Society choice, *Morning Tide* nurtured Gunn's belief that the past had much to offer in terms of being the source of guidance in his search for a vision of renewal and regeneration. Describing the strength and diversity of rural community life in the village of his childhood, the book exudes a freshness and vigour that can only delight. Within the ingredients provided by the vicissitudes experienced by a community living with the dangers of making a living from the sea and the constant sadness of increasing emigration, the book contains a kernel of hope for the future in the life of the boy so central to the freshness and life of the story. Although urged by an enthusiastic publisher for more of the same, Gunn instead chose to explore in his next two books different territory, but this time in the distant past. *Sun Circle* (1933) is a highly imaginative account of the genesis of Caithness during the Viking incursions of the 8th and 9th centuries with the clash of races, Celtic, Pictish and Norse and the interaction of their ways of life and beliefs. *Sun Circle* was followed by *Butcher's Broom* (1934), a fictitious account of the Clearances in the late 18th and early 19th centuries when rural communities were evicted from their lands to make way for sheep farming. This emotive subject is handled sensitively and movingly by Gunn in a way that brings out the acute sense of betrayal of a people by their hereditary chiefs and signals the end of an important part of the Celtic community structure. The two books were to form part of a natural trilogy that was rounded off by the addition of a later book *The Silver Darlings* (1941) set in the herring boom in the early 19th century – a trilogy that charts the fortunes of a people from a stormy and unsettled birth through periods of quiet settlement and brutal dispossession to the success of the their encounter with the sea, and freedom.

The book that changed the course of Gunn's life and literary career was written in 1937 under the title of *Highland River*. The river is the river of his childhood and concerns at one level the exploration of it from estuary to source. The river is also an analogue for a life, and Gunn's quest is to find the source of meaning within himself. Reflected in the story, which is written in biographical form, are Gunn's own childhood experiences of the river and his later journey along its banks and those of his immediate younger brother, John, who fought in the First World War and read science at university at the time of the great advances in nuclear physics. The combined and wide range of experiences gives the book an extra dimension and makes it relevant to the confused and rudderless world of the 1930s. The book, highly acclaimed, was awarded the prestigious British James Tait Black Memorial prize, and on the strength of this Gunn decided to become a full-time writer and live in the country. He had enjoyed Inverness in terms of the opportunity he had had to mix in intellectual circles, participate creatively in the formative years of the Scottish National Party and offer open house to his distinguished political and literary friends.. In an act of bravado Gunn, having resigned from the Customs and Excise Service, sold his house in Inverness and bought a 30-foot motor boat, in which he completed a voyage round the Inner Hebrides. He recorded his adventures and musings in *Off in a Boat* (1938) – a book that captivates both the practical seaman and the reflective voyager alike. It was a dramatic start to Gunn's career as a full-time writer.

With the adventure over, Gunn had to begin the serious search for a house that offered him the peaceful and tranquil atmosphere necessary for creative work. The house eventually chosen was Braefarm House situated in the hills to the north of Dingwall, his wife's home town; there he was to write eleven novels and a series of essays on country life that were restorative reading for the War years and their immediate aftermath. He started by exploring some of the ideas emanating from his earlier novels in settings and milieu totally different from those of his childhood; in *Wild Geese Overhead* (1939) he chose the city of Glasgow and in *Second Sight* (1940) a deer forest and shooting lodge. In both he explored the inevitable clash between extreme rationalism and an intuitive and instinctive approach to living.

For the next eleven years Gunn was in his writing prime; he wrote prolifically and thoughtfully. He was happily settled in a comfortable house which enjoyed a broad open outlook; he had access to woodland, hill and moor for the afternoon walks that meant so much to him; he had the intellectual stimulus provided by the companionship of his immediate younger brother, John, a mathematician and physicist, who lived in a nearby village. Ever the craftsman, Gunn used both his observations of the countryside and his thrilling encounter with nuclear physics through discussions with his brother to colour his essays and novels.

Wild Geese Overhead and *Second Sight* were written during the research and gestation period for Gunn's greatest novel *The Silver Darlings* (1941), a book that completed the trilogy of *Sun Circle* and *Butcher's Broom*; it is, however, much more than a magnificent epic of the herring boom of the late 18th and early 19th centuries; it shows the regeneration of a community displaced by the Clearances and contains within its awe-inspiring descriptions of men making a living in the inhospitable and threatening ambience of storms and treacherous seas the simple and moving story of the intricate and moving relationships between a mother, son and lover. Throughout this enthralling story there is a subtle interweaving of action and metaphysical speculation and a constant feeling of optimism and hope.

Nothing could be more different in physical scope than the book that followed *The Silver Darlings* with its title of *Young Art and Old Hector* (1942). It takes the form of an enchanting dialogue between a young boy and an old man – the present talking to the past. Gunn was to use the pair again as the main protagonists in his Orwellian novel, *The Green Isle of the Great Deep* (1944) – a novel that predates Orwell's famous '1984' by several years. It uses a rural setting rather than an urban one for the struggle by Art and Hector to preserve their individuality and freedom of thought in the totalitarian state in which they find themselves. They emerged from their ordeal unscathed because of their attachment to a way of life that had evolved from the distant past and was still in evidence in their home village. The book was particularly apposite for the 1940s when the totalitarian regimes of Nazi Germany and Soviet Russia were part of the world scene. Between the writing of the two books Gunn had clarified much of his thinking at that time in the novel *The Serpent* (1943). It is the story of an intellectual rebel who returns to his homeland after having lived in the city for a large part of his life and who muses philosophically on all his varied experiences. The setting for this book is the countryside around Braefarm House.

Gunn was to write five more novels and complete a series of essays before he had to leave the Heights of Brae because of the expiry of a rental agreement in 1949. The novels have a variety of themes – murder in a close and remote community and its implications for personal relationships in *The Key of the Chest* (1945) – the return of a failed student to his native community and his rehabilitation and eventual success in *The Drinking Well* (1946) – the escape to spiritual and mental health in the Highlands by a young woman from a blitzed London and Marxist circle there in *The Shadow* (1948) – an archaeological quest that led to the discovery and loss of a crock of gold and the finding of a metaphorical treasure that made life worth living in *The Silver Bough* (1948) – and the escape through an enriching and fortifying cultural background from a world on the brink of nuclear conflict during the Cold War in *The Lost Chart* (1949). Running through all the novels is a thread of speculative thought on a variety of matters such as human relationships, the individual's duty to his community, the aridity of social engineering and the place of the past in human activity as a source of guidance and wisdom.

The expiry of the rental agreement in 1949 marked another turning point for Neil Gunn in his literary and everyday life. The tenor of that life is beautifully reflected in a collection of essays of the Braefarm House years that was published in book form under the title of 'Highland Pack' (1949). The enforced exodus from the landscape he loved and the cessation of a pattern of living that suited him heralded a change of focus for much of his later work. He began a deeper exploration of what he called 'the inner landscape' through selective reading and revelatory experiences in his own life to illuminate his search for self realisation and ultimate meaning.

His next move was to a house (Kincraig) situated off the road between Dingwall and Evanton on the western side of the Cromarty Firth. It commanded extensive views of the Firth and the Black Isle, but it was overlooked and close to the main road to the North. It was not the haven Gunn had imagined as the necessary peace and quiet were lacking. Nevertheless, whilst there he managed to complete a collection of short stories, *The White Hour* (1950), some of which were improved versions of those from an earlier collection, *Hidden Doors* (1929), and a picaresque novel that was both innovative and explorative, *The Well at the World's End* (1951). This novel is a clear exposition of the development of Gunn's thinking at that time and is best described when he himself writes about it. 'Where most novels of the more ambitious kind today deal with violence and materialism leading to negation or despair, I thought it might be a change if I got a character who would wander among his fellows looking for the positive aspects of life. Is it possible to pierce the negative husk, the dark cloud, even for few moments, and come on the light, the bubbling well at the end of the fairy tale?'

In 1951 he moved from Kincraig to the village of Cannich in Strath Glass in Inverness-shire. A stretch of fishing on the right bank of the River Glass went with the large house Gunn had chosen (Kerrow). There he was to write his final three books – all very different from each other. On the surface *Blood Hunt* (1952) is a simple, beautifully balanced story of murder and revenge in a remote and peaceful community. Its fascination lies in a good man's positive and loving response to the events in his effort to preserve the wholeness of the community and eradicate the consequences of the negative and evil intrusion into its life. The second book, *The Other Landscape* (1954) could be called Gunn's *Tempest*; it tackles the impossible, and in it Gunn's metaphysical and aesthetic speculation reaches new heights. The use of the first person by an articulate and interested observer in the novel draws the speculation closer to the reader, and in stronger form. This disturbing novel brings into focus the long distance covered by Gunn in his spiritual pilgrimage through life – from the grim realism of *The Grey Coast* to an intensive search for meaning, self realisation and light in a seemingly uncaring world In *The Other Landscape*.

But the pilgrimage had not ended; in 1956 Gunn wrote his so-called spiritual autobiography, *The Atom of Delight*. This bears no resemblance to the accepted form of autobiography as a series of facts and dates in chronological order; it is simply a random description of experiences and books that have had an influence on Gunn's life. These included an encounter with Zen Buddhism in a book called *Zen in the Art of Archery* gifted to him in 1953 by a great friend who appreciated his interests and direction of his thinking and who was to become one of his biographers. Zen was to play an important part in Gunn's thought processes in the years that followed. In Zen Gunn discovered something he already knew. In the philosophies of Zen Buddhism and Taoism Gunn recognised the moments of perception and insight as aspects he had known an experienced throughout his highland life. After *The Atom of Delight* it was goodbye to books, but not to essays. Those of a philosophical nature and with frequent allusions to Far Eastern philosophy were to become a continuation of some of the themes explored in the autobiography. Essays of a more practical nature were also to flow from his pen.

In 1960 Gunn made his final move to a spacious and comfortable house in its own grounds (Dalcraig) near the village of North Kessock on the Black Isle. It was a well chosen haven with a fine view of the Beauly Firth and access to a quiet road by the shore. He was only there for three years when he suffered the irreparable loss of his wife 'Daisy' who had provided the richly warm atmosphere in all the houses in which they had lived together; she was the gardener too, and this Gunn greatly appreciated. After her death he continued to write articles and essays, one of which is included in this collection. A year before his death in 1973 he was informed by the Scottish Arts Council of the creation of a Neil Gunn International Fellowship for authors of distinction in the English speaking world as a token of the high regard and esteem in which he was held in literary circles and in recognition of his place as one of Scotland's great 20th century authors.

We should like to thank Keith Sutherland for his unstinting support and assistance in the compilation of this book.

1

Why are Writers Nationalists?

Scots Independent, 1940

I am sometimes asked how it comes about that nearly all our best Scottish writers are nationalists.

The answer might take as many forms as there are writers.

For example, the last direct declaration I have read in this connexion occurs in Edwin Muir's distinguished autobiography, "The Story and the Fable":

> Because of this I believe that men are capable of organising themselves only in relatively small communities, and that even then they need custom, tradition, and memory to guide them. For these reasons I believe in Scottish Nationalism, and should like to see Scotland a self-governing nation. In great empires the quality of the individual life declines: it becomes plain and commonplace. The little tribal community of Israel, the little city state of Athens, the relatively small England of Elizabeth's time, means far more in the history of civilisation than the British Empire. I am for small nations as against large ones, because I am for a kind of society where men have some real practical control of their lives. I am for a Scottish nation, because I am a Scotsman.

If out of that wise and characteristically lucid declaration I, as a matter of personal predilection, were to choose any particular word for further consideration, I should choose the word "tradition."

Quite simply, his tradition means much to a writer because only within it can he express himself most profoundly, can he body forth his unique experience as a living creature in the clearest way.

This is not merely true of the great writers of the past—Burns leaps to mind as the Scottish example—but also of our great modern writers.

James Joyce has lived a cosmopolitan life, is a scholar and linguist of uncommon ability, yet his greatest work deals with a day in the life of his native city, Dublin, and into this day is crammed, not only representative happenings and events, but the very essence of the Irish character, released from its background, its history, in rhythms that are Gaelic.

Efforts made from time to time to ignore tradition and write as if we had no past—or so iniquitous a past that it had better be forgotten—have failed.

An organised effort of the kind on a large scale was made by writers under the new regime in Russia, and had to be abandoned. Now great Russian writers of the past—Pushkin, Tolstoy, Dostoievsky, etc.—are being vastly acclaimed in their own country.

I happen to have beside me a copy of the Anglo-Soviet Journal for April, 1940. It deals with some of the arts—the theatre, opera, ballet and music—in the Soviet Union.

In the article on "New Trends on Soviet Ballet," the writer (Joan Lawson) says: "Ballet is essentially an art of tradition, tradition which was handed down from master to master. There is evolution, but never revolution, and because of this the traditions upon which ballet is based cannot easily be violated."

This statement derives not from theory but from experience.

> After the Revolution the enthusiastic young revolutionaries who took up the ballet considered that all the old ideals of choreography, based on traditional technique, should be replaced by revolutionary ideas in movement. All the old themes were to be forgotten, all the canons of ballet traditions were to be broken up and new ideas of dance movement take their place. But with a few exceptions these experiments were found to yield little material advantage. All ballets produced between 1917 and 1930 have gradually dropped out of the repertory of Soviet Ballet.

But the art of ballet – like any other art – may not stand still. In Russia it is receiving a deep and living impulse by going back to folk-legends and folk-dances.

> "All this pre-occupation with ethnographical and historical research will, I am convinced, help to solve aesthetic problems of ballet in Russia, and prove that the future of Soviet ballet lies in a closer attention to the wealth of folk-dance and music …"

I think of our own Gaelic folk music and dances, not in the first instance because they happen to be part of our Scottish tradition but because they deeply affect me.

I grow envious of the Russians.

I wish we could so run our affairs that our unique music would become the intense concern of our musical creators. It never can, and never will, successfully, until once more we re-establish belief in our own Scottish tradition, our own Scottish life.

History shows me that we lost this belief when we handed over our destinies to a people with another tradition. Two traditions cannot emerge. As one becomes dominant , the other slowly dies.

In the drawn-out process, the folk of the dying tradition experience what the psychologist calls frustration. They cannot produce anything creative. They live on their past, on things like Mods and "gatherings." And indulge in the luxuries of gloom and sadness.

In his autobiography, writing of the fine work of our composer, F. G. Scott, Mr. Muir says that though an English singer will, as a matter of course, sing songs in German, Italian and French, he "is unwilling to make the slight effort needed to master the language of Burns, and that language, though it is capable of expressing all the shades of feeling from tenderness to passion, is conventionally regarded by the English as comic."

In a recent issue of *The New Statesman*, an English critic (George Orwell) deals with a Scottish historical novel thus: "It is quite a good story if you can bear the subject, which I admit I cannot … I confess quite freely to a prejudice against books about Scotland …"

That the English audience should find comic what Mr. Muir considers a masterpiece, or that Mr. Orwell may indulge a somewhat heavy honesty over this nuisance of books about Scotland, is merely what we must expect.

They are getting rather tired of us and our precious traditions now. High time that we said good-bye to all that, even should it mean listening to 'Tom Bowling' and Mr. Orwell's prejudices.

We have no one to blame but ourselves. Indeed, I hope I can to a large degree understand and sympathise with Mr. Orwell.

Unfortunately that does not help me, born and bred in the Scottish tradition. And the matter is further complicated by the fact that I cannot completely suppress my own tradition and accept another in its place.

Psychoanalysis has been built up on this matter of trying to suppress a vital experience. In a moment of crisis the suppression upsets the whole bodily and mental mechanism and we have a condition of shock.

In the case, say, of a crashed airman suffering from shock the psychologist finds the cause of the trouble not in the actual experience of the crash but in some long-suppressed and forgotten experience of childhood. And the proof lies in the psychologist's success in dissipating the state of shock and bringing back health.

But there can be no space here to draw a parallel between the individual and his experience and a people and their experience (tradition), nor to bring ample confirmatory evidence from the histories of many countries. Several articles would be needed.

But I hope I have at least suggested the drift of the reason why his tradition is vitally important to a writer and, therefore, why his country, which contains his tradition, must be a healthy, creative, continuing country.

The Essence of Nationalism

Scots Magazine, 1942

In recent times surely more books have been published on nationalism and its horrid implications than on any other subject that affects the destiny of man. A combine of sovereign states to lead and police the world (the dominant-Anglo-Saxon concept); federalism, with its abrogation of certain sovereign rights; a United States of Europe; international Marxism; and so on. Running through the variegated theme is the curse of nationalism, until the ordinary man has begun to yearn towards some vague brotherhood or common-wealth that he hopes may somehow be attained somewhere, and thus a little peace be granted in our time, O Stalin, or O Churchill, or O Roosevelt.

It is all really becoming very confusing. For whereas we read about these grand concepts or pious aspirations on the one hand, on the other we come sharply up against the desperate situation of those who have been dispossessed of their nationhood. For the dispossessed we have immediate and profound sympathy. In Atlantic charters we vow that the disinherited shall once more possess their earthly kingdom.

The trouble with a great deal of this aspirational writing is its essentially idealistic nature. The longer I live the more I mistrust idealism, not for what may be genuinely implicit in it, but for the lengths to which history has shown me human nature will go in order, as we say, to implement it. Let an idealism, with power, once get the bit in its mouth and nothing will stop it. It becomes capable of cruelty and slaughter on a gargantuan scale. Take the Christian religion, with its concepts of brotherhood and charity and non-violence and tenderness, and then consider what man made of it, how the Inquisitor lit the faggots round the trussed-up heretic or the Calvinist uttered his battle-cry of 'Jesus and no quarter'. There you had devastating and most bloody wars, not for declared nationalisms or systems of economics, but for spiritual subjugation or conformity. Christ's non-violence was turned into active violence by that simple process of logic which declared that if all heretics were destroyed Christ's church on earth would be assured, whereas, if heretics were allowed to multiply, manifestly Christ's church would be destroyed. It is the logic that sits in the heart of such apparently fool-proof reasoning that is so very deadly to man.

Even the most cynical materialist, with the strongest aversion for any form or kind of religion, does not attack Christ's teaching as a cause of barbarity and war. What sardonically amuses him is the way man can in words affirm the holiness of such teaching and in practice deny it in order to achieve his own temporal ends, and always with a righteous show of reason.

If this can happen in the spiritual realm, where all our human divisions should presumably be transcended, is it not even more likely to happen in our ordinary working world? In a word, is it nationalism that is to blame for the condition of the world to-day, or is it the interpretation we care to put upon that word when we refuse, perhaps subconsciously, to face up to quite other factors?

Is it not, for example, just a little bit suspicious that most of the grandiose schemes for federalism and what not emanate from America or this country? When you are sitting pretty on top of the world very naturally you don't want things unduly disturbed. How obvious all that has been in a personal way in the ordinary social sphere! The squire's lady sends a jelly to the sick poor or a pair of rabbits to the local hospital. The squire sits on the bench. The laird does his bit in local government. The landlord, in fact, may presently be at the stage where he will hesitate to prosecute a poverty-stricken peasant for poaching a pheasant. If I had land and folk poached my game I am quite sure I should be very annoyed about it. But I might hesitate to go to extremes, if I felt that I might thereby endanger my possession. It is better to concede certain small privileges than to lose the main substance.

Grandiose schemes do not emanate from the peoples of the Continent who have been dispossessed. They have seen 'a new order' at work. All they want is their own country back, their own land, where they may be allowed to labour and produce in peace. They are not theoretical about this or grandiose. They know what they have endured, and they are either passionate in their attitude or bitterly apathetic.

Ah yes, it may be said, but as nationalism is the root cause of all the trouble, something must be done about it or our whole world will come to an end. Someone must do a lot of thinking about it now.

The dispossessed, both in the national and the personal sense, are beginning to question this whole assumption. They have grown tired of theories and want concrete facts. And the biggest concrete fact they can look at is the emergence of Russia.

Now from the Russian point of view war is brought about not by nationalism but by economics. That, we may say, is merely another theory. But at least Russia put the theory to the test within an area covering one-sixth of the earth. She deliberately set about encouraging her nationalisms, and she had a great number of them, different races and different tongues. In this country, for instance, we found Gaelic one tongue too many and authoritatively set about its destruction. We felt it had been and might again be a disruptive element. In Russia different languages were authoritatively encouraged, grammars being specially written for those that had none, and the folk-life in each case was deepened and enriched. Where we saw that nationalism might be a disruptive and violent factor in the whole body politic, Russia saw that it would be a cohering factor, making for peace and harmony. And, whether we secretly like it or not, Russia has proved herself right to a degree that continues to admonish us.

Now this is no veiled plea for communism or any Russian interpretation of it. It is an effort to look straight at this somewhat baffling affair we call nationalism. Whether wars result from basic economic causes we may debate. That some of our bloodiest wars did not result from national rivalries we know. (Consider the recent war in Spain or the religious wars that cut across all nations.) True, nations are used as instruments in war, but then so are scientific research and pulped poetry books and glycerine.

Let me pause to look at this matter in a personal way, for ultimately if we are going to understand anything we must apprehend it not as a verbal theory external to us but as something internally felt and comprehended.

Some time ago I listened in to a programme of music by Sibelius, broadcast at intervals by the BBC. I had not heard any of the Sibelius symphonies before and the effect upon me was something that I could not have anticipated, for it was as if the whole Northland of forest and loch and legend came alive before me, evoked out of the blood. I am neither musician nor musical critic, and could not have been led away by any technical considerations. All I know is that the music had for me an evocative power, some extraordinary element of intimacy. I naturally, I suppose, put this down to some degree of affinity between our Scottish Northland and the Scandinavian, to both a personal and traditional apprehension of these northern lands and seas and the legends or myths bred out of them.

Now the next thing that happened, quite involuntarily, was the thought, flashing across the mind: If only we had a composer who could do for Gaelic folk music and our Highlands what Sibelius did for Finland, how supreme a realm of musical delight would be there! For I happen to know the Gaelic folk music as a natural inheritance and find in it movements of the spirit that no other music can provide, that indeed in some unconditional way make me think are extra-musical, penetrating into that ultimate region where myth is born.

And so the mind came critically alive and I said to myself: What a tragedy that the whole creative musical impulse of the Highlands, as exhibited in our folk songs, should have been crushed and inhibited by certain definite historical happenings! What a tragedy, what a sheer meaningless waste!

In that moment of regret, primarily for my own loss and then for the loss to the world, I touched what is for me the whole essence of nationalism; and, I am convinced, not only for me, but for every normal man who looks into his own mind and refuses to be bedevilled by theories or the power-lust which corrupts. To love your own land, from which you draw your deepest inspiration, is as natural as to love the sunlight or a woman, is to understand what moves in the heart of a Pole or a Czech, is to salute Sibelius not in envy or hate but in admiration and gratitude.

Again, recently, I found myself listening-in to one of Edwin Muir's broadcasts, dramatising Scottish history. He was dealing with Burns and the citations he put into the mouths of the actors were spoken in a Scots that had no slightest suggestion of the comic parochial, but that on the contrary came out of a rich tradition, intellectual, metaphysical, aristocratic in quality and humanly profound. Here was the accent of the ballads, of the Court poetry, of the genius of Burns, of a small but great people making their distinctive contribution to a native culture that in its turn enriched world culture.

It is not my purpose in this short article to discuss origins of war. All I am suggesting is that there are forces at work in the world, of many kinds and of different intentions, directing our thoughts to what are called the evils of nationalism in order that our sight and our reason may get suitably befogged. In times past, as has been clearly documented, private armament manufacturers found little difficulty in promoting a war for their own purposes. That is the simplest kind of illustration.

And just as nationalism could be used by armament manufacturers so it can be, and is being, used by power perverts in an effort at world domination. But they also use pageantry and music and science and every fine element that ever the human spirit has produced to further their ends. But the wise man does not become ashamed of the scriptures and throw them over because the devil quotes them.

3

Nationalism and Internationalism

Scots Magazine, 1931

The other day I happened to meet a Scottish painter and etcher who was kind enough to invite me to a private view of some of his recent work. It was distinguished work, full of vision, and aware of all the ways of the moderns, but by no means the least interesting part of my visit was the artist's own ideas and experiences elicited by, let me hope, natural questions. For example, a couple of his canvasses were concerned with ploughed fields. The serpentine furrow was the motif in a bare Scottish landscape. Not, possibly, what would popularly be called a 'picture'. Yet the artist had been intimately attracted by the subject, and, though believing that the attraction was peculiar and personal, had nonetheless had it included in a group of subjects from different parts of the world for a one-man show. Consider his surprise when the bare furrows caught the particular attention of the metropolitan dealers. It was almost enough to make him conclude that trips to North Africa may be fascinating, but not necessarily essential for the production of masterpieces! And if this theme provided a nearly endless one for speculation at least the one fact had emerged, namely, that by the artist's doing what he knew intimately, and what had appealed to him deeply in his own country, he had attracted the closest attention of art lovers in other countries.

I mention this experience because it happens to be the most recent of many that have, from time to time, seemed to explain to me the relationship of nationalism to internationalism. Nationalism creates that which inter-nationalism enjoys. The more varied and multiple your nationalism, the richer and profounder your internationalism. Conversely, were the nation to disappear and the world become a single body governed by the same machinery of laws and ideas, the common stock of culture would tend to become uniform and static. For cosmopolitanism does not readily breed the intense vision or rebellion of the native or individual spirit. On the contrary, its natural attitude is to deplore it as being unnecessary, often wasteful, and nearly always in bad form. Cosmopolitanism working through this man-of-the-world conception might out of an ultimate logic create its own ideal, but it would be the deathly or neutral idea of the perfection of the beehive.

Now the question arises here:—Why, then, is there in the world of affairs to-day the idea of antagonism between nationalism and internationalism? If internationalism is nationality's flower, why war? And it is precisely in this awful region of war that so many of us lose our bearings. For nationalism breeds patriotism; patriotism, it is asserted, breeds antagonism; and antagonism needs the mailed fist.

But patriotism, as a true emotion, is full of life; it has kinship with poetry and music and none with destruction and death. From the earliest times it has been the world's singing subject. In the history of each nation it has been a unifying and precious possession. Each nation has been prepared to fight for it, when it would not quite have been prepared to fight for its music and poetry, or, indeed, for any other of the mind's preoccupations except religion. Patriotism, indeed, fed such arts as poetry and music. Possibly no other single emotion is more responsible for the creation of the world's culture.

But that sort of patriotism has as little to do with jingoism as music has with a factory siren. And it would be almost as reasonable to suggest that we could get rid of the unwelcome noise of our machine age by first of all abolishing musical scales and musical instruments as it would be to suggest that we could get rid of jingoism by first of all abolishing patriotism. There is no philosophic basis here, and the reasoning is of the kind that has been prolific of so much action, or rather restriction, in recent world legislation. What interferes with our natural love of country to-day may regulate our drink to-morrow, our clothes the day after, and our conjugal relations next year. Patriotism may yet keep us from being slaves—if only of the Wellsian aseptic city-honeycombs.

Patriotism (even already the word is beginning to have a false note) is founded in tradition, and we can no more get away from tradition than from ourselves. Indeed, immediately we get away from tradition we do get away from ourselves. A nation's traditions are the natural inspirations of its people. How much the child is the product of heredity and how much of environment may be a debatable point, but that he is the product of both is unquestionable. Out of his environment, acted upon by a traditional or national unity, he creates most profoundly. And to create is to cause or give delight. In the pure conception of patriotism there is pure pleasure just as there is in any true function of the arts. And it is only when a man is moved by the traditions and music and poetry of his own land that he is in a position to comprehend those of any other land, for already he has the eyes of sympathy and the ears of understanding.

How then has patriotism in idea got debauched by war? Simply because in time of war patriotism is so strongly roused to protect its frontiers that it has been confounded with the cause of war. Nations are the natural units in the war game, just as the family is the natural unit in the nation. But it would be as ridiculous to destroy our natural unities in the hope of destroying the war game as it would be to remove our teeth in the hope of getting rid of a pain caused by our stomachs. For, as has been said, patriotism is never a cause of war, but is merely used by war, just as other emotions are, only more profoundly. For even when nations group into compact empires or into scattered commonwealths, when they lose their nationhood and traditions, war can still use them. War can use them without patriotism. War can enjoy the spectacle of patriots of the same nation fighting each other. War is insatiable, and in the last resort cares nothing for nations. It cares only for destruction, and the earth laid waste would be its final triumph.

Why then blame this creative emotion of love of country as causing war, when we have at long last been forced to learn that war is caused by emotions quite other in origin and aim? We know something now of the appallingly defective system of producing and distributing the goods of life that obtains in the world to-day. Men of goodwill and of all political faiths are being staggered at the dreadful paradox of unemployment, hunger, disease, slums—as a result of over-production. Because we have produced more than we need, we are in danger of starvation! At least the spate of war books has made one thing clear (and particularly the German books), that the peoples themselves had no desire for war, that they feared and hated it as it continued, and that in the largest countries in Europe they smashed their own governing machines in the hope of getting some sanity, some food, and a little peace in their time.

Internationalism carried to its logical conclusion of a single centralisation of all power—arms, finance, law-making—could result in the greatest tyranny the mind of man is capable of conceiving. While the nation is still the unit (and history has shown the small unit to be singularly important—consider Greece and Palestine) the individual factor comes into play, and in a myriad personal contacts the finer elements of humanism are retained and tyranny suffered briefly, if at all. But when the governing machine becomes single in control, remote in place, and absolute in power, then hope of reform or progress—which generally means the breaking of an existing mould—would not have the heart to become articulate. Standardisation would be the keyword not only in the material things of life, but also in the spiritual. And whenever conditions got too desperate it would mean revolution, or world war on a basis of class hatred.

The small nation has always been humanity's last bulwark for the individual against that machine, for personal expression against impersonal tyranny, for the quick freedom of the spirit against the flattening steam-roller of mass. It is concerned for the intangible things called its heritage, its beliefs and arts, its distinctive institutions, for everything, in fact, that expresses it. And expression finally implies spirit in an act of creation, which is to say, culture.

Culture thus emerges in the nation, is the nation's flower. Each nation cultivates its own natural flower. The more varieties, the more surprise and pleasure for all. For nationalism in the only sense that matters is not jealous, any more than music is jealous. On the contrary, if we are gardeners or musicians we are anxious to meet gardeners or musicians of other lands and rejoice when their blooms are exquisitely different from our own. In this way life becomes enriched, and contrast is set up as a delight and an inspiration. To have no longer these means for discrimination, to lose the charm that unending variety gives, to miss the spur in the shadow of difference, "is, on this short day of frost and sun, to sleep before evening".

4

Defensio Scotorum
A Reply to W S Morrison

Scots Magazine, 1928

In the previous issue of *The Scots Magazine* an article had appeared by W S Morrison, in which the writer had criticised many modern Scots critics of Scotland.

The confusion of thought in Mr W S Morrison's article, *Defensio Scotorum*, is such that one must either assume a conscious disinclination on his part to face the facts as presented with such ruthless logic in Mr G M Thomson's *Caledonia* (which he presumes himself to be critically combating), or else consider his article as a sort of impromptu after-dinner oration culminating in the emotional glass-tinkle of 'Highland honours'. England may have her praises incomparably chanted by such as Swinburne, may be made the over-note of the greatest cycle of song in the world, but Scotia—ah, Scotia 'has no classic dignity'. And forthwith our hearts must thrill at the very parochialism of the thought! 'She is to us,' pursues Mr Morrison, 'the old, imperfect, harassed, homely, gallant old dame. Her tartan shawl incompletely confines her grey locks. Her arms are akimbo in defiance of all the great ones of the earth and their works. Her heart is unconquerable and true as steel to her own. "Scotland! my auld, respected mither!"' And involuntarily one looks round for the stirring rumble of the kettle-drums, for manifestly that is the sort of thing to give the tartan troops. ... And here they come, marshalled by *Caledonia*, to pay tribute to their gallant old dame, having inscribed on their banners in letters of fire—45 per cent of us live more than two in a room; we have the highest death-rate, unemployment rate, sick rate, infant mortality rate, emigration rate and immigration rate in the British Isles; for all that spells denationalisation, the destruction of a great tradition, the defeat of a whole people, we stand; our slums are the blackest in Europe, our famous Highlands have become the sporting preserves of English and Yankee money kings …

But the banner legends are too numerous for even irony to dwell on it. Truly it's time the auld mither dropped her 'gallant' shawl, her 'akimbo defiance', and substituted there for the only other attitude she knows, that with the 'tear in her e'e'. In either, one readily grants Mr Morrison, she is not a classic figure. 'The tongues of men and of angels cannot describe her,' he says. And for a moment one wonders what might happen if a lower order of being had a shot at it—though for that matter there is always the kailyaird. Meantime neighbour England, even with the tongues of men, has put up a pretty fair show—Chaucer, Spencer, Shakespeare, Milton, Wordsworth, Shelley, Keats ... down the long splendid line to the Hardys and Eliots of to-day. Yet, for old fact is stranger than new fiction, there was a time, while Scotland was still a nation with her own court and her own poets, when she figured as by no means the least important national entity in European affairs, and certainly as one of the major contributors to European culture—and that, too, at a period when by comparison England was culturally quiescent. When, therefore, Mr Morrison has his gibe at the Scottish Renaissance movement, at Mr C M Grieve's 'Not Burns, Dunbar', he is misunderstanding, presumably deliberately (for in *Albyn* Mr Grieve has put matter and intention clearly enough; and from his article it appears that Mr Morrison has at least seen this companion issue to *Caledonia*) not merely what Scotland did accomplish in her pre-Union history, but what a band of Scotsmen are attempting to do for his 'auld mither' to-day.

But before dealing with this, the most significant, aspect of the attempt to tackle the Scottish problem, let us endeavour to visualise what sort of figure it is that Mr Morrison sees in the Scot whom he is defending. While granting that it is certainly interesting to see ourselves as others sees us, yet we are not in a last resort what others see us (or would like to see us), or indeed in any significant sense anything but what we see ourselves. We are what we are—but what that distinctive essence of us may be Mr Morrison, as a Scot, makes no attempt to discover, either by deliberate personal psychoanalysis or by reference to the cultural history of Scotland, to the supreme utterance of her true artists, to the characteristic actions of her warriors and law-givers, to her varying attitudes under changing religious faiths. Instead, 'there is no doubt that the Scot of tradition possesses the following characteristics. He is "dour" and "canny", in spite of Mr Thomson and those who resent the imputation with all the violence of an inferiority complex.' (A curiously phrased statement implying that Mr Morrison himself subscribes to the 'dour' and 'canny' legend, quite apart from tradition.) After piling up the epithets 'thrifty ... parsimony ... whisky ... sentiment ... energetic in affairs ... patriotic ... fighter ... Burns ... Shorter Catechism' (the haggis and the bagpipes and the other 'half-comic insignia' having been already introduced), he says that these are the points of difference which an Englishman picks out between himself and the Scot. So, after all, it is an Englishman's picture to which Mr Morrison and tradition subscribe? Or is it not?

This Scotch Coamic, like the stage Irishman, is admittedly in a certain tradition of things with which the more complacent type of Englishman amuses himself into a warming sense of superiority, but is he anything *in reality?* The stage-Irishman, anyhow, was very literally shot to pieces all over the bogs and townships of Ireland, as every Englishman now knows with respect, and in the Abbey Theatre, Dublin, I have too often seen, never to be impressed by any music-hall conception of national character, what a renascent culture can do in presenting the Irish character not as others see it, but as the Irish see it themselves, and see it with such truth of vision, such certainty in delineation, excusing nothing, distorting nothing, that when their Players go to London, the greatest English critics are loud in their praise and in their hope that, by reflection, the body of purely English contemporary drama may be revivified. Though even by leaving it at the Scotch Coamic stage, one might have had some sort of image at least, but when Mr Morrison goes on to quote 'other Europeans' to whom the Scot is 'sudden and quick in quarrel' ... 'a reputation of being as fiery in debate as in war', where have the 'dour' and 'canny' characteristics gone? And he finishes the pretty sketch by suggesting that 'the Scot is a sort of caricature of the Briton'—that is, of both the Englishman and himself (at least)! I admit that, with every desire in the world to get to grips with this slippery fellow, he eludes me.

But when presently an attempt is made to place him in historical perspective, the picture becomes even more inept. As a result of the Union, 'two dangers arose. One was that of absorption into the larger unit, with the forgetting of all that makes Scottish History an epic and Scottish nationality a reality. The other was the even more ignoble fate of sinking to the status of a querulous dependency filled with self-pity and jealousy, shrinking from participation in world tasks beyond its strength and solacing its bruised soul with researches into a past when the demands upon Scotland's spirit met with a more robust response.' There Mr Morrison has stated the position fairly, even with an acumen which is all too obviously sharpened by a knowledge of Scottish affairs as they exist to-day. It is in combating these two dangers, still active, that the Scottish Renaissance movement is now concerned; that all the movements towards Scottish Home Rule are directed. All of which labour, however (including the ruthless statistical compilation of *Caledonia*), is merely a beating of non-existent air, for 'both these dangers have been surmounted', says our defender. 'With a tenacity which provokes the mirth of other nations, Scotsmen have clung to one or two national symbols as expressive of their individuality as a nation. One of these symbols is Burns' ... and the other is 'the Shorter Catechism'!

I admit it has the air of an extensive leg-pull, yet the writer is palpably serious. One can only marvel that what provokes the mirth of other nations and draws bitter irony from Mr G M Thomson as a Scot should appeal to the educated intelligence of Mr Morrison as a satisfactory solution of the 'two dangers' which have been inhibiting the distinctive Scots mind, destroying her nationalism, her sense of being a people, and driving her economically into the black death of the slums. Burns, not, it is granted, even as a poet, like Shakespeare—for a writer knows better nowadays!—but merely as a national fetish, and the Shorter Catechism—that Judaic rosary strung in England.

More slippery than ever becomes this elusive Scot—or, to be done with it, are we dealing not with any real figure of a Scot at all, but with the warm post-prandial haze, or, more insidiously, the everyday atmosphere of 'getting on', wherein everything must look encouraging and inviting (and if possible tinct of the comic) so that the mind be comforted and reality shut out? Either that, or else Mr Thomson's uncanny probing for the fatal flaw in the Scots character spelling ultimate national dispersal and death, is the outcome of a true instinct or intuition. And, in spite of Mr Morrison's unconscious corroboration, I am not yet prepared to grant that.

Though I admit that in his economic analysis, Mr Thomson goes a long way to justify his apparent belief. And just here Mr Morrison's defence, in its failure to grasp psychological significance, is in the true kailyaird tradition. He quotes *Caledonia* to the effect that 'Scots are more likely to be found in "scrubby and subaltern positions" than as "heids o' departments,"' 'whereas the chances are that had Mr Thomson desired to make such a direct statement at all he would have had an *or* in place of that *than*. For his manifest point is that the Scots mind finds its whole outlet in aspiring to occupy the salaried and safe headship of a department, now and then succeeding, but generally sitting tight as 'the invoice clerk', rather than adventuring upon the aristocratic—Live dangerously. That the department may sometimes even be the English Government or the English Church does not invalidate the idea, it merely bears it out with a sort of ultimate logic. Indeed, granting—what I think no one will deny—that the Scot has as sound a logical apparatus as any of his neighbours it becomes inevitable, when all his faculties are centred on this 'getting on', on this achievement of departmental security in graded ascent, that he attains to the highest posts on occasion. If he didn't, one would have seriously to question the quality of his brains compared with that of his neighbours'. But to strive for such 'preferment' and salaried safety is perfectly human, if not exactly impressive, on the part of any individual: it is when a nation's whole mind is definitely directed that way, when her educational system, her religious bias, her kailyaird 'literature', aid and abet, that the thing becomes a portent serious and far-reaching. That, I take it, is roughly what *Caledonia* has expressed, though with what inherent truth or falsity Mr Morrison at any rate has not helped to make clear. And immediately one looks around at politico-economic Scotland; all the evidence does insinuate corroboration of Mr Thomson's conception. What is the use of saying, with regard to the admitted horror of our slums, that 'the present poverty of the industrial region of Scotland is due more to the strength than to the weakness of Scottish character'? With every desire in the world to be comforted by Mr Morrison, I can only find such a statement something worse than illogical, almost as bad as his blaming Adam Smith for depopulating the Highlands! If the Scots character was strong enough to make its industrial area boom, why has it not kept it booming; or, when the trade cycle brought depression, why did it not according to its superior strength superiorly keep alive? Where were its 'dourness' and 'canniness', its 'logic and energy when it comes to affairs of government and business'?

But England has had the financial supremacy of London behind her! Therefore Mr Morrison cannot understand why anyone should be disturbed now by the prospect of Scotland's financial centre being shifted to London (there being no Sir Walter Scott with his claymore these days!), or her railways, or presumably the controlling power of any other business: in other words, the complete provincialisation of Scotland is hopefully contemplated, even though it requires no expert knowledge of finance to demonstrate that the belief in any material benefit accruing from the loss of national ownership of capital is an obvious fallacy. It is, in fact, this very process of provincialisation which has brought Scotland to her present desperate economic position.

Her housing, her slums, her unemployment, her mortality, her sickness, stand in black contrast to neighbour England, not to mention other European countries. And it is not a question of the industrial belt alone. Take the opposite extreme—the Highlands. Does Mr Morrison attempt to refute the charge as to the canned meat kings, and such, lording it over a few native gillies and gamekeepers, with the stricken crofter exuding that atmosphere of decay and death, smelt by Cunninghame Graham? Of the boat-loads of Western Gaels shipped abroad like live stock? And as a Scot, a Gael, what action has he taken, or does he intend to take, about it? Does he know the facts, the blue book facts, as to the quantity of land available for cultivation, grazing, afforestation? The Smallholders 1911 Act, with its 20,000 applications and 4,000 grants? That the cost of the last battleship would be about sufficient to buy out on the basis of a twenty years' purchase all the deer forests, grouse moors, and salmon fishings in Scotland? In other words, an annual rental of under half a million would secure the whole lot for the Scots nation. He must know the miserable tale, for the facts are in *Caledonia*, which he presumes to attack.

But as in Mr Morrison's unreal picture of the Scot, with the Comic grinning through, and as in his treatment of the economic position with his only constructive suggestion pointing to the removal of financial and trade centres to London with the unquestionable effect of completing her provincialisation and abnegation of nationhood, so in his reading of her history is he untrustworthy? The Englishman, he says, 'is a unit in a civilisation of longer standing'. What sort of civilisation? And in what way in point of antiquity or culture comparable, say, to the Gaelic?—or Pictish? 'The Scots have never had the impress of any such unifying power, and it is this which renders futile the appeal to Scotland's pre-Union past which is so often on the lips of modern prophets of Scottish nationality.' Has Mr Morrison never read, for example, Mr Evan M Barron's *Scottish War of Independence*; wherein it is shown beyond all doubt that the long struggle culminating in Bannockburn was not a struggle of Anglo-Saxons (Lothians) over Anglo-Saxons as Scottish historians, such as Lang, had hitherto asserted, but a successful war, guided in its beginnings by Andrew De Moray in the North and Wallace (*not* one of the great territorial magnates) in the South, and waged by the common people, the Celtic population of Scotland, against the *national* enemy, England? And as for his statement, 'Behind the Highland Line lay unguessable potentialities of commotion and rapine', it is unpardonable, not merely as historical misstatement by innuendo but as a 'potential' insult to a brave and cultured race in a world as it then existed. The popular belief in continuous inter-tribal warfare is based on myth. That there was such warfare or feuds is true; but then we have wars and feuds to this very day, where commotion and rapine on a vast scale are not unknown; but, as in most civilised countries to-day, there were long periods of peace when literature and music and the arts flourished creatively and at least with a national distinction they have since the Union most sadly lacked.

But if the Scot, his present-day economics, and his history, appear too much for our confused apologist, I can put down the manner in which he has dismissed the contemporary Scottish Renaissance movement only to an ignorance which, being pricked by uncertainty, makes a face of amused contempt. 'Dunbar, not Burns', means for him that we are to sing 'Scottis quhilk hes' instead of 'Scots wha hae'. The crudity of this is appalling, particularly in view of the published work in the Doric of such writers as Lewis Spence, scholarly, classical, and frequently with an inspiration direct as a sword thrust or as a flash of naked colour from one of our old ballads, or Hugh McDiarmid, whose last long poem, *A Drunk Man Looks at the Thistle*, drew from an international critic the considered statement that nothing so great had appeared in English or any dialect thereof for years. These are the beginnings, for this blight that *Caledonia* shows to be resting on everything Scottish has certainly not missed the arts. Artistically in the modern world Scotland doesn't exist. No music, no drama, no letters, of any international significance. Why is this all-round sterility so complete, so without parallel in the life of any modern nation? Should not an honest attempt be made to answer that question before attacking the movement that is trying to do so? If the attempt results in the discovery of a fatal flaw in the Scots character which must result in national disintegration, then with Mr Thomson one may say so, pile up the evidence, and be done with it. But if the attempt results in the discovery that the Scots character, the distinctive Scottish mind, has merely been denied self-expression, has been inhibited and contorted, by ascertainable factors, such as *inter alia*, the loss of government of her own affairs and the acquisition of a too rigid Calvinism and of purely English criteria, then we are up against a proposition capable at least of statement in straightforward terms. For neither does Mr Thomson nor Mr Morrison deny the distinctive Scottish mind. Manifestly, then, in going back to Dunbar, the Movement is merely attempting to get at the fundamentals of

Scottish psychology or character, when that character was flourishing nationally and culturally in Europe, and before it became gradually sterile under these ascertainable historical factors. Mr Morrison says that nationality is 'nothing else but the feeling of traditional tendencies, overriding and directing the eccentricities of individual temperament'. Well, this 'feeling' is precisely what the Movement is attempting to capture in its purity and to *express* and so bring within a living culture once more. It is there in Dunbar. It is not to the same extent in Burns; and, of course, to a vanishing point in the kailyaird successors he inspired. The historical factors have pushed it into a stagnant backwater. At Dunbar (ultra-modern in many respects) we join the main stream again. And once in the main stream our supreme concern must be with the most vital tendencies in modern world literature and art.

In *Caledonia*, Mr Thomson showed the progressive deterioration of the 'Scottish Nation' on all counts. The process is cumulative, and if undisturbed must in the end be complete. Mr Morrison put forward no arguments to counter it. Now the various nationalist movements consider, with a wealth of contributory argument and fact, that the process can be arrested if Scotland be given charge of her own affairs—in other words, if she gets Home Rule. Is there any other way? If so, why not produce it? If not, why the gibe? In the last analysis the basic trouble is a politico-economic one, with Scotland thirled to England and her natural media for self-expression progressively inhibited. We have too much admiration for England and her splendid cultural record to desire to imitate her in a second-rate way. The Scots mind, its distinctive metaphysical twist, its analytical acuteness, its uncompromising realism, its fantasy, its stark humour, its capacity for sheer unconditional vision (consider the ballads), has been blinded, been rendered impotent. When it wins free, as I believe it will win free (the prisoning factor being not a 'natural flaw', but the indicated inhibitions) it will once more take an important place creatively in European thought and culture. But a lot of uphill work has yet to be done by those who love in word and deed this 'auld mither' before that happens; and meantime it is not the Irish who are the enemy, nor Catholicism, nor any other bogey, so much as those whose nationality consists in toasting Burns comically and thrilling to the Shorter Catechism; it is that curious barren defeatist figure, the Anglo-Scot.

5

The Hidden Heart

Scots Magazine, 1928

For those who have listened to the beat of the ancient heart, who know
where the honey of delight is hived, adventure beckons once more—and
perhaps once more to a 'lost cause'—but, once more.

What is that which in our time is making the Scot nationally self-conscious? Is
there some hidden motif beneath all the revealed motives, a core of desire dressed
up for public exhibition in economics and history? If only one could get at that
core, not with any view to helping "the cause" or damning the immigrant, but
simply to feel the heart-beat as a profoundly aesthetic experience. There might
result, of course, more than an aesthetic experience; probably would, or the pulse
had not flushed outward to visible "movements"; but, in any case, to be at the
core conscious that however inexpressible, however hopeless, in an age wrung
pale by materialism, here at last is the ultimate fount of impulse, the veritable
first "cause."

For the principle is always something more than its manifestation; more than,
for example, its economic manifestation. That Scotland should be unhealthy
economically may be due to causes that have nothing to do with nationality
either dead or resurgent; but that Scotsmen should want to stop the 'rot,' should
grow anxious about it to the extent of forming nationalist societies of all sorts,
has an indicative significance. For *at the core* it is not an economic matter at all.
Consider, for example, the possibility of the Highlands under a vast water-electric
industrialism becoming a rich area peopled by aliens (by no means such a fantastic
possibility to those who have studied with some care recent developments in the
West—to the extent, say, of noting the nationalities of those householders of
Kinlochmore called as witnesses in the boundary encounter between Inverness
and Argyll). An alien population producing no matter what riches would so
palpably, so ironically, defeat the Scots idea! Rather, if it must be, the old poverty
with the old race, and the fight for economic betterment going on. So that, finally,
it is ourselves we are concerned with, that something in us which is forever native
and distinguishable; and instinctively knowing this, we flush outward to all sorts

of protective movements or make-believe or even blushes; seldom do we pause to listen consciously for the beat of the heart itself.

And yet this should so manifestly be our first rather than our last or altogether missed preoccupation. For if there is not in the heart a music of life that can stir us profoundly, then any 'movements' towards self-protection are merely instinctive in the animal sense and as such possess no discriminated value, no spiritual thrill. And it is the thrill we want. In the first instance we must be moved not towards societies but to our hearts core. If beauty and courage and intuition of the nameless graces do not sit round the heart of the Scottish idea, warming to its glow in mutual swift apprehensions, then any outward 'movement' is not merely dead show, it is uninteresting and must be sterile. Nor need we be lulled by such words as beauty, spiritual, and their like, for what we are finally getting at is the one individual word—delight.

Considered clairvoyantly, there is this delight at the core of our heritage; and as always with delight, there are the accompanying movements of freedom and charm and a continuous and profound interestingness. It is the delight that inhabits all great art, and, one might add, particularly great tragic art; an exquisite capacity for subtle discrimination that feels and thrills, that penetrates the properties and the proprieties to the central radiance wherein our minds flash as friendly or avenging swords. Yet whether friendly or avenging, still with delight, with a knowing consciousness of the inalienable rightness of our attitudes fronting no matter what greatness of beauty or peril. This (strange heresy!) is to be at ease in Zion—certainly, I believe, in the Scottish Zion.

All of which is rather like a begging assertion of what ought to be at the core of the Scottish idea Well, let us see; and the only place to get the right view and the proper perspective is in history. Personal 'sentiment,' the personal confession of faith, does not readily convince the Scots mind which at the slighest intrusion on its privacy so readily turns to intellect and metaphysics.

What, then, is Scotland's historic background? Against what natural stage setting do we comport ourselves with assurance and freedom, importing significance to the slightest gesture, the least stressed exclamation? Unquestionably it is Celtic—in that racial sense in which Celtic is not so much opposed to as set against Teutonic, Slav, etc. Now one is aware of, and can sympathise with, the feeling that this 'racial business' is overdone. It provides no small source of humour to a mood grown materialist, sceptical, a trifle weary; but whenever the mood in a vitalised moment craves the innermost thrill of delight, then the racial distinction is at once there and fundamental. See how excitement reveals a man's nationality, making it leap out of him! And culture is an infinitely more difficult thing to satisfy than excitement; it is, as it were, excitement become a conscious art. To get, however, a distinct single view of this Celtic background, and at the same time to lift it by a sort of parellelism to that plane where we need not stare ourselves too closely in the face, I should like to point to that extraordinary book by Daniel Corkery called "The Hidden Ireland." This book deals with the Irish who lived beyond the Pale in the eighteenth century. It shows, with the impartial historian Lecky, the terrible condition of the peasantry—filth, famine, the plague, and death with the green munge of nettles about its mouth. Outcasts dying off under a penal code which offered no slightest chink of hope to effort howsoever heroic, which denied them land-ownership, the professions, education, their church, with the infamous system of rack-renting tearing them remorsiessly on its wheel. The picture is one of the gloomiest in all history. Then Corkery penetrates beyond Lecky and the other historians and lifts the veil from what is surely one of the most wonderful instances ever recorded of racial persistence in its highest aspect. For these half-clad, bare-foot, starving peasants were the heirs of a culture a thousand years old and they had never forgotten it; nay, more, they practised it, and that in its highest manifestation, in poetry and music, and found therein their only, their last, solace. Were this not sufficiently documented, it would be incredible. But there it is, and the author has so lived his theme, that with final understanding has come a quietude that rarely rises to a gesture, as though before what the eyes see and the heart knows any striving 'to make a case' would be an adding of the meretricious to the lees of irony.

His attitude to that eighteenth century of Irish history is in a way curiously like the attitude of Pater to the Renaissance (though with what an illuminating difference the Gaelic Corkery regards the Renaissance with its "whitening" of native cultures!). There is indeed a wistful note, just as there is in Pater when he writes of Joachim du Bellay and the *Pleiad;* in each of them a lingering preoccupation with, a reiterated insistence upon, the graces and refinements of a perfected technique. For from the immemorial Bardic Colleges had come a tradition of poetry written with absolute attention to form and style, to rhythm and harmony; and when these colleges—the lay universities of Ireland (as also, of course, of Celtic Scotland)—got broken up by those whom Swift dubbed 'the conquerors,' then the bare-foot peasant poets, from their fever huts and their stoney fields, met in what they called their Courts of Poetry, and there contended with one another, not so much in 'making poetry' as in improvising variations on a given theme; not as strolling singers or artless versifiers, but as masters of language delighting in the artist's use of their medium, in delicate inflections, in subtle assonances, in fleeting gleams and shades, threads of harmony woven into a sound-sense that stole away the senses. One quotation from this absorbing book may perhaps be hazarded. When Owen O'Sullivan writes his friend to put a handle in his spade, he couches the request in lyric form; of which a Gaelic verse is Englished:

'At the close of day, should my limbs be tired or sore,
And the steward gibe that my spade-work is nothing worth,
Gently I'll speak of Death's adventurous ways
Or of Grecian battles in Troy, where princes fell!'

'Labharfad féin go séimh!' ('I myself will gently speak')—as if he said: 'I will put off the *spailpin*, the earth-delver, and assume my own self, the poet!'

In evolving the Courts of Poetry, in maintaining them, the literary tradition of the Gaels did its utmost to ensure that its legatees should, at least on occasions, assume their higher selves, their fuller humanity, should put off the mere delver of the earth, should raise themselves, should extend themselves to the contemplation of the adventurous ways of Death, or to the vision of the burning towers of Ilium....

It is a story without an equal in the history of literature.

And this preoccupation with technique, the artist's love in his skill, that can only come of a great tradition, an old culture, may be seen to-day in the Irish poets who, working in English, are so conscious of their heritage; in the poems, say, of F. R. Higgins, who in a note appended to his 'The Dark Breed,' writes of the younger Irish poets imposing on their "English verse the rhythm of a gapped music, and through their music we hear echoes of secret harmonies and the sweet twists still turning to-day through many a quaint Connacht song. For indeed these poets, in the lineage of the Gaelic, produce in Irish lyric—with its exuberance arid wild delicacy—the memories of an ancient and rigorous technique." And again.—"The racial strength of a Gaelic aristocratic mind ... its poetry is sun-bred; twilight for it is just the tremulous smoke of one day's fire. Not with dreams but with fire in the mind ..."

That, then, is a view of the Celtic background, essentially Scots as well as Irish, no matter how historic accident be juggled. The Bardic Colleges of both countries used indeed an identical language, a literary Gaelic, set above all local dialects (do we hear in these days of 'Synthetic Scots!'). And the tradition extended for a thousand years. When Dr. Johnson said that there wasn't a written word of Gaelic more than a hundred years old, how the impulse provoking the *niaiserie* is deftly illumined! Against this immense Celtic hinterland our modern mechanistic culture and Teutonic drift is a slight thing. This immemorial heritage has become part of our unconscious self. When influences combine to inhibit its liberation, then we grow dissatisfied and grope around for 'movements' as for weapons, for kilts and memoried Bannockburns and jokes, hoping to lull ourselves into a sceptic irony or a visionary satisfaction.

But, it must be insisted upon, in the last analysis it is the *quality* of the heritage that matters. And in Celtic culture as it throve throughout Scotland and Ireland from prehistoric times there is, above all else, a constant recognition of the inalienable dignity of man in face of the eternities, of all that comes between birth and death, of love and beauty and peril, finding outlet in poetry and music, in the carving and decorating of valour's shield, in tribute to all those attitudes and aptitudes of the mind that made of the halfclad peasant an aristocrat in. his own right. And even in these latter, days in Scotland the ancients spirit manifests itself in divers ways, in (more typical, perhaps, than all else) the instinctive desire of its people for education, for learning, for those university degrees that, as it were, symbolise possession of the ancient rigorous technique of the bardic schools. Not easily does the leopard change his spots. The Scot is essentially a mental animal.

History is not an affair of one's yesterday and to-day; its waves and recessions are slow and august. The dissatisfied Scot may be feeling back for a potency greater, more imperatively needed by humanity at large, than he knows of. His stirring to a sense of receding nationality may also be an instinctive reaction against a world-wide gathering of mechanistic forces, his Celtic unconscious rebelling against the tyranny of the iron wheel.

True, it may sound therefore a rather fantastic exaggeration to say that in saving himself the Scot may assist at saving the world. The machine has made us too clever by half, and a wheen of us too comfortable, to be much more than the negatives of a 'realist' grin. Yet for those who have listened to the beat of the ancient heart, who know where the honey of delight is hived, adventure beckons once more—and perhaps once more to a 'lost cause'—but, once more.

6

Scotland a Nation

Left Review, 1936

In the *Left Review* for last February, Mr. James Barke has an article that is by far the most searching piece of criticism on the late Lewis Grassic Gibbon that I have seen. In the beginning of that article, where he has occasion to contrast my work with Gibbon's, he writes, 'The identity of Gunn's Nationalist ideology with that of the Aryan theoreticians of Hitler Fascism is not so fortuitous as its superficial form and expression might indicate.' This was an aspect of the matter that had not occurred to me, possibly for the reason that my knowledge of the work of the Aryan theoreticians is even less than my knowledge of the intricacies of controversy. Perhaps, therefore, some sense of ironic humour should stop me from going on; yet as my interest in Scottish Nationalism is shared in varied form by a great body of the Scottish people, it is possible that my particular attitude may have for your more confirmed readers at least a curiosity value.

My first difficulty with the proletarian as with the racial theoretician is his penchant for absolute categories. Because I may have been concerned with Scotland and the Gaelic form of civilisation Mr. Barke classifies me as 'idealist,' and because Gibbon was 'consumed with the vision of Cosmopolis,' Mr. Barke sees him as a 'materialist.' Now it seems to me that anyone who is concerned with a vision of a new social order must logically be concerned with ideal speculation, whereas one dealing with a given nation and its known social or cultural factors must in exposition be essentially realist or materialist. It may be held that the whole special doctrine of dialectical materialism was telescoped into the word 'materialist.' Even so, that could not fundamentally alter my contrast, while it would endanger the use of language as a medium for the communication of individual thought.

Now the basic idea in the Scottish Nationalist movement is that Scotland is a nation, precisely as England or Germany or Russia is a nation, but that by the Union with England she lost control of her nationhood, became governed by the English parliamentary and financial system, and so has been rendered incapable not only of helping herself, but of taking a direct part in any world movement. I am aware of how the word nationalism may offend the nostrils of wholehearted proletarians, of how the word nationhood may be as outmoded as last seasons favourite slang word in Mayfair. But I may not allow such emotional reactions here to cloud the fact that in the world to-day the nation is still the instrument of social experiment. Recently the French nation went Left and immediately set about making and enforcing such laws as suited its ideology. If Scotland went Left tomorrow (even now in Parliamentary votes she is majority Socialist), she could do nothing about it. At Westminster she would be outvoted by eight to one. And if she decided on revolution—though she has no national mechanism even to permit of such a decision—she would be immediately and automatically overpowered.

That a violin may be made to produce the most excruciating noises, that strychnine may be used for murder, explosives for war, are hardly in themselves sufficient cause for the abolition of music, medicine, and mining engineering. That a nation may be used by capitalism, Fascism, or Socialism, hardly implies the need for abolishing the nation. If the nation is the actual instrument by which the proletarian theory is being put into practice in the world to-day (as it is—and the only one), then to deny the instrument out of some vague zeal for its international manifestation would seem to me an act of desertion and cowardice in the proletarian struggle. Scottish Nationalism explicitly has nothing to do with Communism any more than it has anything to do with Fascism. Its fundamental aim is to reintegrate the people of Scotland into a nation so that they may then, according to their lights, work out their own destiny and assist in working out the destiny of the world. For them not to do this is to abdicate in the human struggle, and represents incidentally an acquiescence in national self-destruction without parallel in the history of the world.

All that may seem very obvious. But its pith, for my purpose here, lies in this, that it compels Scottish Communists into the category of theorists, makes them lookers-on or hangers-on in the proletarian struggle, their destiny to conceive of themselves as educational or intellectual apostles to the English. Bernard Shaw said that the first thing to be noticed about Stalin is that he is a nationalist statesman. And it would seem reasonable to suggest that if Stalin succeeds in the Russian experiment, the fact of that success will be a thousand times more powerful in its effect on the workers of the world than all the theorisings and plottings of the Communist intelligentsias in all the capitals of Europe. For Stalin to endanger his experiment, or to lengthen the time of its fruition, by wasting his force in extra-national intrigue, now that he is *in the process* of turning theory into practice, and with sufficient elbow-room and resources to do it, would arguably be a tactical mistake of the worst kind, both to his immediate purpose and to the realisation of the full Marxist doctrine.

From recent happenings in Russia, it would appear that Stalin is aware of this, aware of how some purely psychological factor like the 'will to power' may act on those divorced from a specific job of work. Yet though I see him thus clearly concentrating on his national effort, it would not occur to me to align his 'national ideology' with 'Hitler Fascism.' And Lenin, however he may now be held by the orthodox to differ from Stalin on the vexed question of the primacy of national or international action, did in fact not only use Russia the nation for his purposes, but inside Russia herself also encouraged the re-birth of old nationalisms with a practical and cultural success that recently drew high tribute from Ernst Toller.

So much for the nation as an instrument.

Now, apart from the satisfaction it gives the normal man to work within his own nation, it presents him with a 'closed area' where theory may most readily be translated into practice. I am aware that many readers of this *Review* may expect me to show that Scotland is still a nation of sufficient worth to the world to wind up and get going again. For the world can use its past only in so far as it is of value to the present and future.

But this is an impossible task in a short essay, though, given a little space, it might be a fascinating one. It would not only begin by showing that Scotland is one of the oldest nations in Europe, and, I believe, the only one that was never conquered, but would, for the earliest times, have to delineate a society that functioned on a communal basis. But not a primitive society as that phrase is usually understood. It had, for example, a highly developed literature—an art-poetry as well as a folk-poetry. It had different orders of poets. When this Gaelic polity was converted to Christianity, it sent its scholars over Europe. (All this would throw a revealing commentary on some recent Marxian impatience with anthropology.) Out of it came a social consciousness that can be traced in all distinctively Scottish institutions to this day. For instance, in his Gaelic commonwealth the land was communally held and the responsibility of rulers and officials was downwards to the people: in direct contrast to the feudal system where responsibility of the rulers was upwards to the king. The feudal system came in with English influence and vitiated the native system; yet the native system was so inbred that as late as 1886 the crofters, fighting on the old idea that the land belonged to the men of the clan, by a remarkable agitation forced the Westminster government to pass an Act conceding security of tenure and the fixing of an economic rent by an impartial tribunal. In religious government the same tendency may be traced. Scotland still has her own legal system. And so on.

But this ancient belief in the importance of the folk went deeper than a natural tendency to form democratic institutions, for in its social manifestations we come across all sorts of interesting communal expressions, such as the folk music that accompanied folk labour. In other words, this Gaelic society from which we in Scotland have emerged is the only one which imbues for me the superficially vague expression 'proletarian humanism' with a deep significance.

Mr. Barke talks of 'a Gaelic culture revivalist' distilling 'from the Gaelic past something of the quality which he believes to be the dominant racial quality of the Gael: an aristocratic, individualist quality.' And he may be right. What he may not quite have understood is that the 'aristocratic, individualist quality' is not inconsistent with an extreme belief in the folk, but in fact may be implicit in it. If Communism isn't going to abolish the haunting fear of economic want, and so free the individual to indulge his powers of aristocratic discrimination on any plane he likes, then it doesn't seem to me worth discussing.

Accordingly, what I fail to understand is how Scottish intellectuals of any persuasion, and particularly the proletarian, are not prepared to accept this historic past subsumed in this country of their own and attempt therein to make a concrete contribution to social reconstruction in the interests of the folk. Their historic background and educational facilities—if there is anything in the idea of dialectical materialism—equip them for the task in a way undreamt of by the Russian mass, and should enable them to short-circuit the more obvious crudities of dictatorship and bloody violence. Anyway, it is a job of work. But they fly from it and cover their desertion by calling the Scot who would like to attempt the job a Fascist. Marx knew the primary value of practice. He also strove to make it clear that in his theories he envisaged living working men, not economic abstractions. But when we avoid the concrete job in front of us in order to go theorising internationally, no wonder we become 'consumed with the vision of Cosmopolis'—that typical bourgeois vision that Wells has made all his own, and which is not merely the negation of the 'aristocratic, individualist quality,' but surely a conception of a beehive tyranny unspeakably repugnant to the free-thinking developing mind.

7

The Gael Will Come Again

Scots Magazine, 1931

The previous month's *Scots Magazine* had carried an article, 'Celt and Norseman: A Contrast', by Alexander Urquhart. The latter 'extolled the industry, adaptability, and hard-headed tenacity of the Norseman in his profitable development of lonely island settlements to the belittlement of the Celt, with particular reference to the [then] recent St Kilda evacuation.' The following was a reply to Urquhart, 'a defence of Celtic tradition, and a declaration of the present-day potentialities of that tradition.'

That Mr Alexander Urquhart in his article on 'Celt and Norseman' has unjustly overstated his case against the Highland Gael does not, as he may feel it would—or even should—rouse that picturesque figure of his fancy to immediate fiery wrath.

The dignity, 'frequently indistinguishable from the silliest form of vanity', may, when it exists (and where doesn't it?), be affected. That is about all. Why? Just because of that element of truth underlying the trenchancies of Mr Urquhart's charge, an element seen by the true Gael himself more than by any other. This is not a matter for sweeping comparisons and violent accusations. One may be down at heel and yet not a fool. In the world of affairs it is a commonplace that the predatory instinct triumphs over the spirit. Nor need we slip on platitudes. For what has long happened to the north-west of Scotland is now perceived as happening to Scotland as a whole. There has been an insidious process of decline, throwing up the usual symptoms, which Mr Urquhart observes in the case of the dreamer with his 'humbug', but may miss in the case of the Scot with his haggis. It might be interesting to diagnose these symptoms, but it would probably land us in the wide region of national life and affairs, where the external simplicities of Mr Urquhart's observations would neither explain nor reveal very much.

His comparisons with the Norse may be, for example, entirely misleading. It is possible that on one of his islands a thousand miles north of the Hebrides a colony

28

of Gaels might thrive (and so repeat history), and that on St Kilda, because of those very contacts with 'civilisation', a colony of the hardiest Norsemen might in a generation or two ask a beneficent government to help them 'to conquer fortune' (a fine phrase!) by removing them to the mainland. Any Saxon business man whom I have met would indeed consider such a move for such a purpose a natural and wise one. So that when Mr Urquhart is being ashamed over the St Kildan exodus, I feel that his shame is really not so much for Celt or Norseman as for human nature. And we all have our share of that.

Perhaps that is why Mr Urquhart cannot find the cause of the 'lethargy and slackness' of the west, though he is satisfied that it lies not in race but in the language, nurture, and tradition of the people. That is about as vague a statement as even a dreamer could make! It is, more unfortunately, an illogical one. For as Mr Urquhart asserts, at one time St Kilda carried a population of 200, who throve on the results of their own labour. I make no doubt they throve as well as did any contemporary Norse settlement similarly placed. They were also, according to travellers, given to the social arts of singing and dancing. And of that self-supporting colony, a remnant of 86 was evacuated recently and the island abandoned. Yet it was the same language, an unbroken tradition; and, in the same environment, there were presumably the same potentialities for nurture. The 'slackness and lethargy' cannot therefore be implicit in these three factors. The cause must be searched for elsewhere.

Nor is St Kilda the solitary example. The mainland was also in time past inhabited by a self-supporting people, who gave a good account of themselves not only in social life and the creative arts of poetry and music, but also in the matter of personal daring and courage. They not only fought with distinction in the wars of Europe, but took a hand in making history at home—and if they had then developed, in place of their marked individuality, this new art, which Mr Urquhart observes, of 'leaning' on each other, it is possible that that hand would have been a decisive one. But in those days there was, alas! less 'leaning' amongst them than amongst their enemies, the Saxons, who also, of course, had numberless more shoulders for the purpose.

The language, tradition, and nurture of the Gael sufficed in those days, and would have sufficed in these, if they had not been interfered with from outside. I am not now referring to tourists' tips nor charity's tinned meats, though these maybe are all that trouble the facile minds of travellers to-day. The root-cause is deeper and more desperate. It struck at language, at honour, at livelihood, at tradition, at their arts and amusements, in a way that for stark brutality is without parallel in modern Christendom (Ireland not excepted, that other home of the Gael). There is no space here for the petty details, though their tone might be given by quoting from the oath which a Highlander had to take after the '45. It refers to the charming matter of the pattern of the tweed he wore. This is what the Sheriff asked him to repeat:

...and never use tartan, plaid, or any part of the Highland garb; and if
I do, may I be cursed in my undertaking, family, and property—may I
never see my wife and children, father, mother, relations—may I be killed
in battle as a coward, and be without Christian burial in a strange land, far
from the graves of my forebears and kindred; and may this come across
me if I break my oath.

The people were not only 'cleared' out of the glens, hunted and dragooned, or
shipped abroad like cattle, but those who remained, after being cowed into a
mood of utter subjection, were by the most subtle and insidious means, religious
and educational, made to despise their language and tradition (nurture now
barely arising).

From such a gruelling onset, pursued in various guises through generations, a
people does not recover all at once. It takes time. 'Lethargy and slackness' are not
perhaps unnatural. Even 'dirt and squalor' might be expected. Tinned jellies are
acceptable, and a little Celtic-twilight is imported for sleep.

I would pray Mr Urquhart not be intolerant and, before the Gael has quite
come to himself, threaten him once more with a Norse invasion.

Also I would ask him, when he finds so certainly that the Gael's 'affinity to
poetry and beauty' is 'all humbug', to inquire into the matter beyond the personal
chance encounter. He would not, I presume, call the glorious record of English
literature 'all humbug'—after spending a day in Clapham.

Gaelic poetry and music are no myths. There were dialectal differences all over
Gaeldom, but scholar's Gaelic was common currency in Scotland and Ireland
until the seventeenth century. Gaelic literature was in its flower centuries before
the beginnings of English literature. Dr Johnson was revealingly ignorant when
he said that there was no Gaelic MS over 100 years old. There is indeed such a
wealth of Gaelic MSS in existence that one savant suggests it will take 200 years
for Gaelic scholarship to deal with them. And as a Gaelic poet of to-day says of
this literature as a whole: 'Its poetry is sun-bred; twilight for it is just the tremulous
smoke of one day's fire. Not with dreams but with fire in the mind ...'

There might well be then the 'lethargy and slackness', but what there has
been is passing before the slow but sure uprising of a new confidence. As for Sir
Archibald Geikie's 'squalor, dirt, and laziness', I can but suggest that the learned
geologist was singularly unfortunate in his encounters, just as any foreign visitor
would be unfortunate who got his idea of the Lowlands from the Cowgate or
the Cowcaddens. But Gaelic history is proverbially the comment of the outsider.
Lecky found conditions a thousand times worse in the Ireland of his day—even
if, incidentally, he failed to find at the same time the existence of the 'Courts
of Poetry'. The Gael under the pale was certainly at his social lowest. He had
lost heart, and was living in conditions utterly appalling. But he lived through
that infamous time, and to-day is running his own affairs in a Free State that is
financially about the only one in Europe approaching complete solvency.

In my experience of the west I may have been more fortunate in missing the 'squalor, dirt, and laziness', and finding instead hundreds of homes, humble enough materially, but at least with the graces of hospitality and a natural courtesy. The exception occurs everywhere—and here need hardly be a concern for our scorn in the face of history.

Finally, Mr Urquhart's preoccupation with his Saxon ideal of the go-getter is interesting as a personal expression but not conclusive as a way of life. It has hardly, for example, landed the world in a golden age completely devoid of poverty and squalor. In the midst of plenty (called over-production), we suffer the grisly spectacle of famine. Against the tyranny of the machine and the predatory instincts of the go-getter, new conceptions of life and work are needed. The Gael in Scotland may have had 'inferiority' drummed into him, but he will come again—only, in his own way, which may not be the way, however admirable, of the 'humdrum Saxon', nor, perhaps, will the world lose by the distinction.

8

A Visitor from Denmark

Scots Magazine, 1937

Arne Ström, the Danish writer, called on me the other day. He had worn out a pair of shoes tramping Skye. He had talked to fishermen and crofters wherever he had gone. 'Here and there a black-faced sheep!' and his gesture conveyed, with a dry smile, our agricultural condition. 'You hard-boiled individualists!' When he wished to convey irony, he generally indulged in American expressions. For he had left Denmark to go farming in a big way in America. He had been through the period of depression there, when farmers at the end of desperation had shot their stock and sometimes themselves. But his specialist knowledge of poultry had helped him through, and finally had procured him a commission from the Soviet Government to be foreign adviser or expert on one of their huge poultry farms (1932-33). The story of these experiences he has told, I believe, in one of his books. He is not only a man of wide experience, but of the shrewdest practical under-standing, caring far more for describing precisely what he has done and seen than for theorising about national politics.

I mention all this about him because of the conclusion he had come to after tramping our Highlands. 'Had I known this lovely country, had I seen it when I was twenty, I would not have gone to America. Never. I would have come here. I would have taken one hundred Danes with me. We would have set up a colony. We would have worked in co-operation. We would have done well. Not any men, but the Danes, who know how to work. And their women. For, on a farm, the woman is everything. She makes it.'

But he was too old for that now; he was forty, and a correspondent on a leading Copenhagen newspaper that had sent him to Scotland to report on our economic conditions. Did Scottish newspapers pay correspondents to go to Denmark to report what was being done there in the way of co-operative farming? Could I tell him the name of a book giving a complete and impartial survey of crofting and sea-fishing in the Highlands? Could I—? But to all his questions I could give little more than a confused negative. There were odds and ends, pamphlets, day-to-day journalism about things, I suggested haltingly. He smiled. 'This Caledonian Power Scheme?' and he eyed me, politely not wishing to commit himself until he saw to which side I belonged, for he had already tumbled to our partiality for wordy fights rather than for constructive work, for opposition rather than for co-operation. To him all the talk seemed so sterile a waste when—here and there a black-faced sheep!

His English was good, but clearly he would have liked now and then to have let himself go in his native tongue.

Perhaps, however, the restraint was even more impressive. He could hardly, he suggested, with smiling irony, explain to them in Denmark. He dare not. To explain what could be done here—if we worked—if we under-stood how to work—ah! that might be so successful that we might threaten the Danish market in this country. Certainly. It would not do. And I realised that he would in fact be discreet.

We walked, and I drew from him pictures of Denmark. The Denmark of a couple of generations ago, newly conquered by Prussia, Schleswig-Holstein taken from her, her farming going down before the great grain-bearing lands of America. A Denmark defeated and in despair. Then the power of the idealists, who taught them two things: their history and new ways of farming; the nationalists who said, we need faith in ourselves, in order that we may work for our own and the common good. These pioneers of the 'School of Life' inspired the simple farm labourers with stories of their country's past. They met and talked in farm kitchens, somewhat after the fashion of the Highland *ceilidh,* yet different from the *ceilidh* in this, that the tales of the past were matter of inspiration for the present and the future. They were mocked. But they persevered. They increased in numbers. Farmers met these new co-operators with pitchforks. But the ideal was strong, for it was not only based on faith but on knowledge; it was prepared not only with words but with deeds.

And out of these simple beginnings came the co-operative system of Danish farming that has commanded the admiration of the world; and, in a sense, the even more remarkable development of the kitchen *ceilidh* into the Folk High Schools. We pride ourselves on our education in Scotland. Make the most cursory examination of what Denmark has done for her working young men and women in her Folk Schools and then proceed to comparison. At this moment a student from Scotland may take the international classes in the school in Elsinore for the three months, April-July, at a total charge, including board and lodging, of £14.

Denmark is little more than half the size of Scotland and carries a population of some three and a half millions. A fifth of the country is peat moor or sand. It is flat and without metallic ores, coal, or water power. Yet these Danes, inspired by love of their own land and carrying the ideal of brother-hood in labour into the severely practical business of co-operation, have made of their country one of the most fruitful in the world. The nationalism out of which this magic has been wrought cared nothing for armies and navies and Empire. It concerned itself with the creative work of men's hands; it satisfied the aspirations of individualism while directing these aspirations towards the common good; and when personal needs were thus ordered, it continued organising these adult schools through which the mind may attempt to realise its spiritual potentialities.

I began to understand, as Arne Ström went on talking, the background to his thought, and to apprehend, if dimly, how the Highlands must appear to him. He had been picking up facts about unemployment: 25 per cent in Inverness-shire; 40 per cent in Ross. Were these figures true? Were the Highlands indeed classifiable as a distressed area? And our sea-fishing: it seemed to be in a bad way, too?

I knew most of the relevant facts. It was not easy talking. I did not care about repeating what I wrote here in the March issue on pauper lunacy. The picture seemed dark enough without referring to an unnecessary emigration, to a declining population, to an increasing dependence on dole and State money. As we walked out of Inverness, I thought of the crofting lands in front of us towards Beauly and of schools there where half the children are Glasgow orphans boarded out by the Poor Law. Where was the old virile life of this particular area, once the most fertile in the North? What had happened? What was wrong?

I turned to Ström and asked him how he could be sure, if he did bring his Danes here, that they would in fact work hard and in co-operation. I suppose I wanted to challenge him. But, after a first glance of astonishment, he laughed. It was merely inevitable that they would work in co-operation; just as no doubt it was inevitable that in a town like Inverness there should be a common water supply. It was the best way and it worked. The Danes *knew*.

But I saw that it went deeper than that. Here was an assurance, an optimism, that sprang from some root we had lost. And so real was it that it would never think of expressing itself in terms of brotherhood or idealism, but simply in terms of commonsense. The practical note was uppermost always.

It was difficult for me to put up any sort of case for the existing condition of the Highlands. It seemed futile to try to explain it by a reference to history; to suggest that the `Forty-five and its barbarous aftermath may have started a process of breaking the spirit of the Highlander that the Clearances completed; to show the sheep farm succeeded by the deer forest, tragedy succeeded by apathy. One is reluctant to explain this to a foreigner, not merely out of pride but out of the hopelessness of making it sound reason-able. For the Danes also had had their dark period, but they had come out of it triumphantly. When America and Russia had made grain-growing uneconomic, they swung round to dairying and pig-rearing; they changed the whole nature of their agricultural policy.

But had the common folk done this spontaneously, or had they been inspired by leaders? And the all-important answer was that they had been inspired by leaders. Behind this extremely practical issue of farming and real education, we find the idealists, the men who wrote and spoke of their country because they loved it, who ousted the fashionable German and Latin tongues by the Danish speech of the people, who created and directed the new ways of life, out of which in due course a considerable literature and a more considerable science were born.

Did our trouble lie in this, then—that we had never produced our own leaders? Leaders in all ways of activity and thought the Highlands had produced, but never to express themselves at home. For action, they had gone to London or the Colonies. Administrators, governor-generals, explorers, pioneer farmers, down to political careerists and heids o' departments. Surely out of the long roll the Highlands could have retained one or two for creative organisation in the glens and on the sea—men with vision and patience and belief, who recognised the value of their old culture and ways of life, and who, like these Danes, might have inspired the people to their own economic and educational salvation? For by so doing, they would not only have *created* something for themselves but also in the process have added to the riches and knowledge of the world, as Denmark has done in her example of co-operative small-farming and Folk Schools. Of what value to the Highlands have Scottish Secretaries of State been, or to the world, or to anything positive at all that we can think of?

The best always being drawn away to London or the Colonies. None remaining to organise or inspire. Festive Highlanders boast of the great men they have exported. I ask myself: (1) Has this greatness ever achieved the *creative* record of the Danes who stayed at home; (2) does farming in Alberta or place-hunting in Whitehall make up for a derelict Highlands? If the Danes had aspired, let us say, to departmental seats in Berlin or a 'place in the sun' abroad, would Denmark have the importance she has for herself and for us to-day?

These questions may sound rhetorical. They demand an answer for all that.

My friend returned to the Caledonian Power Scheme again, because he had seen our local press full of it. Did our press also deal with the far greater problems of agriculture and fishing? Did all these local papers use the same heat, fill the same number of columns, over the condition of crofting and unemployment in the Highlands? I was compelled to admit, I am afraid, that they did not. I could not recall any heat or controversy over the desperate position of the fishermen in the Moray Firth ports or indeed anywhere on our Highland shores. Not only was this by far our greatest industry (apart from the land), not only was it hopelessly in debt and steadily declining, but the very basis of its polity—the brave old tradition of skipper-ownership—was in this moment passing away. While nothing was being done, and little said. True, there were Government offers of loans, but on terms so impossible to the defeated men that the irony would be laughable were it not so tragic.

Even the Caledonian Power Scheme—a trumpery affair economically compared with land and sea—could not be investigated on its merits on the spot, so that men of Inverness and men of the Highlands could see exactly what it would mean to them. No. Deputations, after working up antagonisms to each other, must proceed to London in order to carry out, whether they liked it or not, a lobbying of members of the House of Commons on a scale and with an intensity that made of the realities of the situation a farce and must have been to those concerned a deep indignity. And finally the English members who knew nothing about the Scheme, and Welsh members who wanted it for Wales, combined to throw it out.

There is no leadership, there are no men of vision and knowledge. The heat and the controversy are over local jealousies. How could I explain to the Dane that there are folk who do not want industries, who never trouble over the state of crofting and sea-fishing, who are comfortable themselves and therefore wish nothing to be disturbed, who talk of the salvation of the Highlands through tourists impressed by the beauty of empty glens—an attitude by no means confined to Tory reactionaries?

We proceed in our motor cars to these glens and sniff their ozone and express our pride. Yes, this is our country. Lovely, isn't it? We do not disturb ourselves by reflecting that the motor car is a product of a complicated industrialism. We must not let the thought of industrialism taint our delicate Highland nostrils. Oxy-acetylene may be useful for shipbuilding and Highlanders may have proved themselves amongst the finest seamen in the world, but that we should have a factory for its production here—what a polluting thought!

How explain all this to a Dane, looking with covetous eyes at our water power?

And when it comes to the cultural side, how could I tell him that against his Folk High Schools and Agricultural Schools (these are additional, of course, to the ordinary school-university system) we had—the Mod? The Mod as a creative factor in the flowering of our Gaelic heritage! But despair here is too deep even for irony. Meantime Norwegian scholars are fitting out an expedition to find what is left of Gaelic before it dies. Though, as I write this, a newspaper states that Gaelic is not nearly so dead as all that, because our greatest Gaelic lexicographer—a Russian—is just reported to have said that it may last a couple of generations.

Ah! the romantic Highlands, the aesthetic appeal of the glens, the bens and the heroes, the blue waves rolling by Barra and all the haunted Isles; ah! Tir nan Og, och-nan-och, and the songs of the seals! Is it too much to hope that some day this sort of thing may stick in our gullets, that we shall be roused to make it an indictable offence? This parodying of great beauty by the sentimentalists who think factory work ungenteel should fill us, not with laughter, but with shame.

Though what can be said of the jeering opponents of the twilight sleepers, the hard-boiled fellows who allege that the Highlanders are not dreamers but, on the contrary, extremely practical folk who know on which side their bread is buttered? Triumphantly they point to a 100 per cent grant from London for some section of a road as evidence not merely of the quality of Highland leadership in local affairs but of the thereby proven need for retaining the existing regime and its connection with London. After all, we were perhaps a trifle hard on the song of the seal.

Denmark, with her increasing population, could spare a few of her adventurous spirits, just as a healthy Highlands could—and did in time past. But, as things are, it was difficult for me to point to the Highlands and then suggest to Arne Ström that there was something rotten in the state of Denmark! There was, however, one regret that we shared in common—and that was that Ström and his hundred Danes had not in fact come to settle in the Highlands.

9

A Footnote on Co-Operation

Anarchy, 1968

In this age we get so bedeviled by slogans, labels, and schemes in the head, that we forget the realities underneath. Herring Boards or any other kind of Boards imposed from above will do no earthly good unless the producers themselves combine in some sort of union or co-operative. So combined they will then be in a position to take advantage of the Boards or of anything else that comes their way. If they are not combined, spoon-feeding by a Board will keep them going for a time, but in the end, when the spoon-feeding is withdrawn, they will collapse before those who have united whether on a private capitalist basis or otherwise.

That's the simple truth, and the economic history of the Highlands in recent times proves it. Facts about the decline in sea-fisheries, crofting, hill-sheep farming, and so on are known. Equally known is the success of certain northern European countries where co-operation among the producers was the basic order and help from governmental sources the natural result.

But when one mentions co-operation, folk here shake their heads. They either think it can't be done in sea-fishing and crofting or else they get tied up in hot arguments about the SCWS and the private trader.

Never mind all that. Co-operation simply means that small independent producers, threatened by syndicates or great combines, will ultimately be done down unless they come together in a combine of their own. I am not discussing the ethics of this. I am merely stating what inevitably happens.

Now by coming together in a league or co-operative, they can not only hold their own on the economic front, but they can also retain in large measure the ways of life and freedom which tradition and environment have made precious to them. If they don't want to be 'wage slaves', they needn't be. But they have got to come together. Co-operation is a coming together in their own interests.

My friend, Peter F Anson, has recently been in Eire studying fishing conditions round the coast. He has a wide knowledge of the sea-fisheries of Europe, and has surprised me (and possibly himself) by finding an Irish Sea Fisheries

Association which arranges for the provision of boats and gear, co-operative marketing, and other enterprises. In the *Fishing News* he writes:

> All fishermen members are required to enter into a Co-operative Marketing Contract under which they share in the general scheme of the Association for the sale of catches. In some districts it has been found possible to guarantee members, on a seasonal basis, fixed prices at the port of landing for their catches of white fish, plus, when conditions are good, a bonus on their earnings. The Association maintains a boat-building yard and motor repair shops, and in fact does every constructive thing it can in the general interests of the sea-fishing industry.

I knew pre-war Eire fairly well, and all I can say is that if the Irish can do that sort of thing at home, a co-operative association is no dream for Scottish fisheries. I regard self-government for Scotland as co-operation on the national level.

It was the Eire Government that set up the Irish Sea Fisheries Association. Would that Association have been in being were Irish affairs still run from London?

But I do not wish to raise any argumentative issue here. The simple point I want to make is` that individual producers on sea and land will have to combine if they are going to win through. The debt on our fishermen-owned Scottish drifters before the war was as real as was the ever-increasing power of the English drifters owned and run by shore syndicates. History will repeat itself, unless we undertake to mould it nearer to our interests and desires. We can do so; but it means *doing*, action, on a basis of association or co-operation.

There is no other way that I know.

10

The Family Boat

Its Future in Scottish Fishing

Scots Magazine, 1937

No more certain indication of the desperate condition of the herring-fishing industry could be found than in the recent insidious press campaign against the Scottish system of family-owned boats and in favour of the English system of company-owned boats. Responsible fishing opinion in Scotland is satisfied that the campaign was officially inspired, though direct evidence is naturally difficult to obtain. This may be a political point and therefore not to be pursued here, though there are so many parallels to precisely this sort of attack in Scotland's economic history that at least Northern opinion may be forgiven its apparent assumption of official inspiration. The truly insidious nature of the attack lies in this: it is known that the Scottish boats are heavily in debt; if to this fact could be added the idea that the Scottish system is uneconomic compared with the English, then. not only a Government department, but banks, ships' chandlers, and private individuals would hesitate to finance such a system and its ruin would be inevitable. Discredit a man or a system in so subtle a way and his or its doom is written, economic collapse being hastened by the very despair that overtakes the human factors involved. Evidence of this truth may all too readily be found in practically every port on the east coast of Scotland at the present moment.

The Scottish Herring Producers' Association resisted this attack strongly in letters to the Ministry of Fisheries, the Secretary for Scotland, and the Fishery Board for Scotland, and produced facts and figures designed to show that the Scottish system of individual ownership compared favourably with the English company system. If the Scottish boats made a smaller number of landings per boat during the English fishing season, it was because, unlike the English boats, they did not go to sea on Sundays. And if the average shot was smaller, this again had to be offset against the fact that in the given period (6 October—28 November 1936) the English boats had fished on Sundays during October and on Saturday and Sunday nights during November, and accordingly must have landed considerable quantities of overday's and salted herrings. 'The present system of individual ownership in Scotland is not doomed to extinction,' declares the Association, 'and will never be replaced by company ownership.'

It is a valiant declaration, but even in the moment of making it the Association is aware that 'the English boats are backed by capitalists, who may keep on making losses, hoping to recoup themselves later on by the extinction of some of the individual Scottish owners, whose capital is tied up in his boat and gear.'

And therein lies the real danger. 'The cold truth is that from 1931 to 1934 herring boat-owners, both Scottish and English, made considerable losses. There was an improvement in 1935, and again in 1936, but the English-owned boats have no more surmounted their difficulties than have the Scottish.' True; but being 'backed by capitalists', they are more likely to surmount them, because they are better able to last the desperate pace.

The large company can always smash the small individual in any sphere of industrial effort from the local multiple shop to the foreign market. Moreover, when it comes to any such test of endurance, many factors other than the purely financial automatically align themselves in favour of 'big business'. Let me illustrate with a simple instance. There is more than one fishing port on the Moray Firth where fishermen's houses were condemned because they did not comply with local bye-laws regarding sanitation and cubic airspace. The humane local authority accordingly proceeds to build 'council houses' for those affected. The fishermen move in, but find that now they have no lofts and outside sheds for storing gear, painting buoys, or mending nets, as they had in the old homes. Result—they have to pay for storing their gear and for having it mended or repaired.

It may be protested that surely such a position could have been foreseen. I suggest that it might be an interesting exercise among the factors that manipulate our local authorities to discover why it never is.

Or take the case of the men who have cut their losses and gone in for the motor-engined boat and seine-netting for whitefish—an individual enterprise. I have talked to the best of them on both sides of the Firth and already they foresee the end. The slaughter of immature fish has been enormous. The grounds are getting less and less fruitful. Drag after drag often produces nothing of value. They are naturally tempted to poach within the three-mile limit. Many of them are already prepared for any workable system of restriction or regulation that would ensure a reasonable. future for the catching of 'flats' and other white fish. But all they actually see in front of them are foreign trawlers in the Firth (where British trawlers are prohibited) swinging round on a three-mile radius and systematically cleaning the grounds. They have no feeling of security; no conviction that the Government will ever interfere to protect their interests against state-subsidised foreign boats or attempt in any way to assist them with grants or wise organisation. When the Government votes 1,500 million pounds for the defence programme it forgets about the drifters and trawlers, though the Admiralty used over 2,100 of them in the War. All that colossal sum for destruction, yet not one penny for the solitary part of the defence arm that in peace time is productive! It is reckoned that the Buckie fleet in the last fifteen years has lost over a million sterling. And to-day Buckie fishermen, the majority of whom are unemployed from November to June, have the pleasure of watching Danes landing fish at their home port.

Perhaps the basic trouble is that in Britain the fishing industry is not sufficiently organised—in England of not sufficient value—to be of importance in the political game. If Scotland had to deal with her own affairs, her fishing industry would at once be of major importance in her economy, and she would very soon be compelled to give it the attention that the Germans, Danes, Swedes and Norwegians give to theirs. Consider how energetically the Scandinavian countries, for instance, deal with the foreign trawler! But as things are, trouble on the London buses takes precedence in the minds of our Westminster legislators. Though that is less than the truth, for I have been unable to trace any Parliamentary discussion of the fishing industry throughout the life of the present Government. And as for the Herring Industry Board's plans for the reconstruction of the herring fleet, these 'moneylender's terms', as they have been aptly called, it is difficult not to agree with the fish-curer who suggested that their terms were meant not for restriction but for destruction.

Now in the absence of the staying power of shore capitalism, in the neglect of the Government, in the competition from outside by the state-subsidised foreigner, in the impossible nature of the Herring Board's financial offers, and finally in view of the crippling burden of debt already piled upon the Scottish drifter, it is difficult to feel as sure as the Herring Producers' Association apparently do that the Scottish system of individual ownership is going to stand the pace against the English combines or capitalism. For even at the worst, it is not a straight fight. Whenever the individual gets into debt he enters a region where the manipulator of finance begins to make his power felt. If you buy up my IOU's, you can smash me. The case may not be so direct and simple as all that, perhaps, but the principle is the same, at however many removes it may now be operating. The directing power of the English combine in Scottish fisheries is steadily growing. And there is a suggestion of over-strong protest in the statement by the Herring Producers' Association that is at least indicative of the trend. Not panic yet—but the trace of fear.

That is roughly the position, and for the Scottish herring fishing—and white fishing, too—it may well be a tragic one, and not only in the smashing economic loss to those concerned, but in the loss to our country of a system of work and craft requiring the finest human qualities. For though the Scottish system was built on the national love of individualism (stigmatised by some of our country's critics as her fatal bane in these days of capitalism or totalitarianism), yet this individualism always worked towards the family and communal good. This is a fact that cannot be too clearly emphasised. Within it, indeed, lies the suggestion of any contribution Scotland might make to world affairs to-day, for all her ancient institutions do show this concern for the rights and initiative of the individual coincident with the larger concern for the community. The skipper of the typical Scottish fishing boat has always been not only owner of his vessel but one of the crew, who called him naturally by his Christian name. He is one of themselves, one of a small company working for their common good, with powers of leadership and decision vested in him by necessity of their calling. Because of their common religious beliefs, for example, it would not occur to him to go to sea on Sunday—nor would any outside power compel him to go, whatever the material loss involved. To the dangerous business of the sea, he and his crew bring not only the anxious desire for gain, but also their beliefs and decencies, all the human factors that give to man his integrity and dignity. History shows that there have been no harder or more fearless workers in the world, but they have always carried their individual judgments of right and wrong with them. And this, I suggest, is of some significance in the world at the moment. For the problem as I see it is this: how to manage efficiently the economic machine and at the same time retain the maximum amount of individual freedom. The Scottish system of family-owned boats represents perhaps the only great industry left in the world to-day where some attempt at solving the problem continues to be made.

To contrast the English capitalist system of boat ownership, where skipper and men are like so many factory hands under orders from shore, would take too long here, though some day, by way of sidelight, the whole story of the Hull trawlers, directed by wireless under the ruthless demands of 'the market', may be told in all its dreadful detail. I know about it only at second-hand, but if half of what I have heard is true, then the stories of sociological novelists about the more infernal aspects of our city life would make, by comparison, merely pleasant Sunday afternoon reading.

In their fight against the English capitalist system, the Scottish Herring Producers' Association should be supported by every Scot who still has any care for individual liberty and decency. The Association itself should muster all its strength, organise it, approach Scottish MPs, compel their active assistance, and hammer at Westminster. I fear they might not get much out of Westminster. Nothing, if we may judge from the past. But in the process they might get a lot out of themselves, and in particular a clearer vision of where Scotland stands *vis-à-vis* Westminster. This is no veiled Nationalist suggestion. The matter is far too vital for it to get lost in political moves or prejudices. Though I am prepared to offer the Association this tip—if they come out with a strong demand for Scottish self-government, even threaten to join the National Party, they would get more attention from Westminster in ten days than they have got in ten years!

Assuming, however, that it was possible to get from any Government two immediate vital needs: (1) cancellation of existing boat debts and reasonable provision for new boats, and (2) proper protection of home fisheries together with active concern for foreign markets, would the individually owned Scottish fishing-boats be then in a position to face up to English capitalism or Continental subsidies?

They might for a time, but again, as I have suggested above, they would in the long run be on the losing side, simply because they would not have the backing and resources to tide them over difficult times. What further step, then, in organisation could they take so that, while retaining the principle, with all it implies, of 'family boats', they could at the same time be in a position to meet English capitalism or foreign subsidy with a combine of their own.

I suggest that the answer may be found in some system of co-operation similar to that which has proved so successful in Scandinavian countries. Co-operation implies duties and restrictions, but such duties and restrictions would be imposed by the fishermen themselves for their own good and not in the interests either of shore capitalism or of state control. If this were done on an inclusive scale, then they would find themselves in a superior position to the English combines for two reasons: (1) they would not have to provide profits for a capitalist organisation ashore, and (2) they would continue in their own interests to look after their own gear in a way that no driven wage-hand ever does.

With regard to (2), let me quote again from the Scottish Herring Producers' Association's letter: 'It is a well-known fact that the figure for upkeep of nets and management expenses for an English boat is on an average about £350 to £400 in excess of that for a Scottish boat. The Scottish fishermen have no management expense for their boat, no cost for storage of gear, and no shore staff to look after their gear. The fact that the nets are owned by them makes them more careful than the English fisherman in the handling of gear at sea.'

There is truth there, though it must not be forgotten that the English shore organisation does at least keep the boats going, while often relieving the fishermen themselves of many hampering tasks. With fish on the grounds in a short season, it would help the Scottish fisherman to know, for example, that, should he be unfortunate enough to lose his drift of nets, there was an organisation ashore that would rig him out again under conditions that his brother fishermen and himself had co-operatively agreed upon.

Co-operation in this way would be merely an enlargement, to meet modern conditions, of the old communal way of running affairs that is at the root of Scottish institutional life. Once they got their system properly organised and functioning, it would be extremely formidable. If Orkney can make three times her agricultural rental out of her own co-operative way of selling eggs, is it beyond hope that the Scottish fishermen with their great traditions and renowned fishing grounds could make shift to get out of debt? Cooperatively organised, Scottish fisheries would overcome English capitalism, and with a Government prepared to fair play on the international market, they would not need to fear even the state-subsidies of foreign countries.

11

Sea and Land — and Finance
The Church's Great Silence

The Healing of the Nation, 1930

It is becoming easy to read of an emigration from Scotland of 367,000 in the last eight years, of an unemployment rate that has been consistently very much higher than the English rate, of slums that can hardly be worsted in Europe, of a vast immigration of other nationals, of the invasion of our towns by English stores or multiple shops, of the increasing control of banking, railways, and big business from London, and generally of the relegation of one of the oldest and proudest kingdoms in Europe to the condition of a beggared province.

For we get used to statistics. So used to them that we doubt their facility. We see people living around us, going about their business each morning, we see the grass grow, the crops come on, and indulge ourselves by feeling aggrieved at the daily news of the hundreds of thousands who draw the dole for doing nothing. Why not get *them* to do something also? And having intelligently propounded so wise a question, we turn to the sceptic who shows us that anything can be proved—and disproved—by statistics; and particularly to the expert who says that everything is the result of "economic law." To go further in our investigations would be presumptuous.

And, by way of illustration, let us take the fishing industry.

A tour of the coast line of Scotland is a tour of scores of derelict harbours and. creeks, every one of which was at one time tumultuous as a healthy hive. What I have so often seen as a boy comes back: the boats, the East Coast skippers, the Gaelic crews, the women gutters, the curers' agents, the brown sails going out at evening—most lovely of all sights, except perhaps the sight of them coming in at morning when excitement and anticipation quicken tongue and eye at the great gamble of the sea. And, with success in the gamble, how the news spread! So that an old woman of the hillside would cry to a young man passing hurriedly on the little road, "What news to-day?" and the young man would reply, "When I left, Duncan Cormack was in with thirty crans. There's like to be a big fishing." And after a sweet pause, she would exclaim, "Isn't it God's blessing!" The young man would hurry on, smiling to himself at the old woman, smiling out of his excitement and the need for hurrying with the horse and cart, for likely as not there were ten to fifteen shillings in it for himself that day. The shopkeepers would begin tidying up their premises, for debt as well as cobwebs might get a fright before long. And so the whole district was stirred to a maze of happy ordered work, laying up honey for the winter—and fun and the ceilidh and cards and football and games and the "literary society."

Now in that particular harbour, which in its heyday fished two hundred to three hundred boats in the season, there are five small boats—of the type of the old haddock-boats of the winter fishing. The harbour walls, the pier head, the breakwater are sinking and bulging and rent. The basin is silted up. The cooperages and curers' premises are roofless, their windows boarded. Even of the legion of flashing gulls, only a few are left to cry disconsolately and whiten the last remnants of scentless tar and pitch.

The picture could be filled in by tracing all the actions and reactions of the community's life as a result of this brave industry of the sea, and not merely along the lines of material well-being but, more profoundly, down the hidden ways of emotional and spiritual experience. For the central conception is that of young manhood and womanhood in their prime, with on the one hand old age proud of them, often dependent on them; and on the other childhood and youth looking towards them with the secret desire to emulate. For passion was there, and life, and creation.

Before all of which the "economic expert" becomes impatient, muttering "Sentimental!" For it is so clear to him that, however satisfactory "all that" may have been at the time, it is no longer suitable to the conditions of our day. A sailing vessel had only a restricted range. She was bound to go under before steam. Why? Obviously because steam can take a larger boat farther afield, can shoot a bigger drift of nets, and can reach a rail-head port with a greater catch for an earlier market. These small fishing communities were therefore bound to be squeezed out. Fishing must concentrate more and more in the great fishing ports like Peterhead, Fraserburgh, Wick, Lerwick, Kirkwall, Stornoway, etc.; and must go on concentrating still more as drifter competition increased. The small harbours and creeks represented a phase in the life-history of an industry. Their usefulness has passed. They have accordingly died. It's no good being sentimental about it. That's the end of them.

That, anyhow, is the argument, and it looks, in the phrase of this machine age, fool-proof.

It may be, for all that, only the proof of a fool. For the acid test of results compels us more and more to suspect our economic expert. Big-business, attended by financier and publicist, are the trinity we worship to-day. Like Napoleon, they move armies. Human beings become "hands," misery, starvation, disease become "unemployment," a nation becomes a "tariff," and the dread scourge and tragedy of war an affair of "markets." Nor might one fight against this dehumanising process if big-business could show itself successful at its own game; if it could, in a word, distribute the material goods of life. But does it? In our Scotland, with its bare five millions of a population, we have at this moment nearly a quarter of a million out of work. That is the damning answer. Big-business has become the mumbo-jumbo of our industrial jungle; the great financier is its medicine-man; and what we fondly cherish as our emancipated minds are frightened to ask questions and demand realist answers. Even back in the ancient Gaelic commune we find simple food and clothing, perhaps, but no poverty, leisure but no unemployment, neither vast riches on the one hand nor the nightmare of "the backlands" on the other. The great Gaelic heroes worked about croft and creek, hunted hill and glen, exactly like—and with—their neighbours. As a way of life it was logical and effective. And with so little on the plane of material riches (*i.e.* without the aid of the machine), what a large spiritual life was there!

With the aid of the machine to-day (which, it has been calculated, multiplies the labour of one man by at least two hundred), and the unlimited resources of land and sea (for our present poverty is not in *production*, actual or potential, but in *consumption*), we ought to be princes in our own right. But what happens is something like this. There is a machine being worked, say, by four men. A gadget is invented whereby the machine can be worked by one man. Result: three men are thrown out of employment—with the whole appalling train of events from lowered vitality and disease (slums and C3 population), to the ultimate hunt by the machine-owner for foreign markets—and inevitable war. Yet what common sense would expect to happen when the new gadget was introduced would be, that the four men would become approximately four times better off (leaving the term "better off" to be defined in working hours, or machine-product, or both, together with its application to industry as a whole and to society).

Every age hankers after its own strange gods. We have become not only fatal and sentimental regarding ours, but we have also of course developed the necessary jargon. So that any man who questions is smiled at, not merely by the expert but by *the admittedly ignorant*. The modern industrial system, governed by an absolute Finance, is believed in and worshipped ten thousand times more firmly by humanity to-day than all the faiths of all the Churches put together. And our Church, the one spiritual organisation left to us, never questions it.

It not only does not question it; it condones, and that in the most insidious of all ways, for it asks us to accept poverty and slums and suffering as manifestations of the inscrutable will of God; nay more, to accept them humbly as "visitations" by a Divine Power—which presumably might otherwise run the danger of being flouted by a people grown over-confident because they had food and clothes and social happiness in abundance. And if the Church denies this implicit attitude, how are we to find out that it has any other, when it is silent in face of the awful facts? The other day, for example, thousands of baskets of fresh herring were thrown into the sea outside a Glasgow that has tens of thousands of its people perpetually on the brink of starvation! Does it sound a crude question to ask if that was the will of God or merely a flaw in a human organisation? But even crude questions must be asked of a body that before such an appalling waste, amid such appalling human destitution, does not even venture a timid, Why? When the harvests of sea and land are richest, the harvesters themselves are threatened with penury. The other year a bumper American wheat crop was partly used as fuel. And as with the food products of sea and land, so with the raw material and manufactured products of industry. Think of a world suffering unemployment and destitution because of over-production of the very things it needs! The people, as it were, are dying for lack of bread because the wheat crop was so bountiful that, not being an "economic proposition," it had to be burned. Can unreason or insanity go further than this? It can, very much further, for our business men solemnly "explain" it on the basis of financial "laws" (as if they were laws of Nature and unalterable, instead of being the tabulated observations of a financial system quite arbitrarily created by man and as arbitrarily capable of alteration); and our spiritual leaders "explain" it on the basis of God's inscrutability!

It may be a sin to take the name of the Lord God in vain, but surely it is hardly less than a blasphemy to hold Him guilty of a world of hunger and social horror, when He has actually created a land and sea teeming with such riches that, worked upon by man and his inventions, are demonstrably capable of providing humanity in abundance with all that is necessary for perfect physical well-being and social happiness. It is not that what we require cannot be *produced*; it is that it cannot be *bought*. And money is created not by God but by man; to be precise, by the banks.

All of which may be considered a digression from our concern with fishing, but very pertinently is not so. For, as has been said, Finance is the nerve-centre of an economic polity that, having failed in results, must be regarded with a fearless, an active scepticism. And when we revert to a consideration of the concentration of the fishing industry in big ports, "proved" to be so inevitable, what do we find is already happening? That for large and expensive drifters to go great distances to sea to meet herring that would come to our coasts in any case—and too frequently not to meet them at all—is proving under the existing dispensation not merely a failure—which was all that worried fishermen half a century ago—but a creator of the far more grisly thing called Debt. The "solution" to the fishing problem has not been found. It is apparently further away than ever, so far away that it is in danger of being found again in the small boat and the small creek! A certain Moray Firth harbour that has not had a fishcurer for nearly a generation is this year curing again, and fifteen small-type boats, with auxiliary motors (and weekly running expenses of about ten shillings per boat), are doing very well on the inshore fishing.

Here, it would seem, are the beginnings again of the healthy communal life I have tried to describe. What it needs to support it are vision and organisation, not so much on a local as on a national scale; that is, on a scale and by an authority capable of questioning the sentimental or fatalist doctrines of existing financial accountancy, and sufficiently realist to insist that the human factor is more important than a book-keeping entry. The moment is vital in every way. Governing factors like trawling and territorial limits have to be firmly handled and clearly defined. Dutch trawlers can cut up and destroy our fishermen's nets in the Moray Firth openly and with impunity. Scotland contributes a tremendous annual sum to the upkeep of the world's greatest Navy. A futile little patrol gunboat is seen on odd occasions to crawl up the Moray shores. Representations to Westminster have, of course, had no effect, and the fishing banks of the Scottish coast, both east and west, are being continuously raided and destroyed by English and foreign trawlers.

True, the fishing industry is immensely more important to Scotland than it is to England. That is one reason, no doubt, why Westminster had never any hesitation in breaking with Russia. Deputations and appeals from the Scottish ports proved fruitless. And the Russian market, that took 75 per cent. of our total pre-war curing, was denied us. May we be excused for asking why? for whose benefit? under what system?—while the fine men and women of our fishing communities passed away, to the usual accompaniment of economic shibboleths, and a life interested and emotional and spiritual passed with them. But at least the word "Russia" did rouse the Church—to inveigh against Bolshevism and its reported new marriage laws, and antipathy to Christian ritual and dogma, while it failed completely to perceive the stupendous Russian upheaval as a signal portent of the mental unrest and spiritual sterility in the youth of the world of to-day, in the youth of Scotland, youth that for ever hates sterility, and is for ever quickened by the spirit.

And as with the sea, so with the land. The story of the land clearances in Scotland is one of the blackest in history. Always the people have been forfeited to Mammon—but in this matter how brutally! More brutally even than in the congested industrial areas, because at the back of our land communities lies our heritage, a Gaelic heritage for the most part common to all Scotland, a heritage that was cultured and lettered centuries before the first halting articulations of English. Are not its poetic and musical remnants becoming fashionable? Have we not Celtic twilights and pretty-pretty abortions of a Gaelic aristocratic culture? —that once upon a time absorbed Christianity, and sent its scholars to convert half Europe.

But we have dropped our heritage, our true national life, for that charming shy thing called an inferiority complex. The tartan was forbidden, an oath of "loyalty" was made infamously humiliating, and cargoes of Gaels were shipped abroad like cattle.

And now we have a million and a half acres of arable land within the deer forests. There are still some eight thousand applicants waiting for small holdings (with the Government this year hoping to give entry to eighty-nine!). In agricultural circles it is being realised that small holdings pay where large farms do not, for they are worked on a different labour principle. For the Highland type of small holding an outrun is essential. That involves the whole question of deer forests and sporting rights generally. For the Isles, the sea is the outrun. That involves the whole question—very acute and even bitter in certain centres—of ineffective government supervision of inshore trawling. With productive land and sea you have—or, rather, could have—afforestation on a great national scale; while Nature is steadily pouring away almost infinite resources of hydro-electric power.

Scotland is potentially a rich country, and where she is organised she succeeds. Take even the remote treeless Orkneys. Last year (according to an eminent member of the Land Court) the Orkneys exported £200,000 worth of eggs, or four times the total agricultural rental. Yet Scotland has to import eggs on quite a vast scale from China! But apart from such an odd example here and there, organisation is completely lacking. Indeed, according to many, the only hope for the northern half of Scotland is the tourist traffic!

For sheer futility this would be laughable were it not so tragic. Study what has been done in a land like, say, Sweden, where a national government, proud of its country's traditions, has encouraged to success afforestation, hydro-electrical development, and agriculture. There are, for example, over a hundred factories dealing with peat moss. Or study Denmark for co-operative dairy farming. Or even what the Irish Free State has already done for its dairy produce.

The facts and figures can be got easily. What I am concerned with here is the spiritual principle behind them. For the chaotic condition of the Scottish body politic and economic can be but symptomatic of the condition of the Scottish soul. And when in Scottish history we have touched the soul we have usually touched the Church.

What is the Church doing at this most crucial moment in Scotland's history, when it looks as if not only the true culture of our race were passing, but the very race itself? What fight is the Church putting up, not for itself as an organised body, but for that far greater thing, the traditional distinction and freedom of the Scottish spirit? One cannot read of the "clearances" and think kindly of a Church that largely found in them a temporal benefit. What about this more hidden but possibly more deadly because final "clearance"?

The thinking young men and women of Scotland in art, in business, in letters, in politics, have decided to put up a fight for their ancient nation. Even their National Party should be regarded by an acute observer as a profounder thing than any mere political organisation, because it is an outward manifestation of a state of spiritual urgency and need. The economic argument is stressed because the spiritual argument is paramount; because it is known that if the body dies the soul passes.

And we don't want the soul to pass. While it is just conceivable that in fighting for the soul of a nation we may be fighting for the soul of the world. Palestine and Greece were small countries. In her past, Scotland has always shown a pre-eminent concern with mind. Her old literature, her educational systems, her folk-music, the very way in which she, more than any other country, was caught in the toils of a metaphysical Calvinism, go to show this. Subtle debate by crofter and fisherman on a point of doctrine may for a time have inhibited art and sent humour underground, but it had its own insidious delights. We are a mental people, instinctively fitted to fight for the mind's freedom whether against the thraldom of a foreign institution or an international machine.

And in this fight that has now started are the young men and women going to look towards the Church, or, as in Russia, are they going to turn away from it and jeer? Many of them have been asked what they would like the Church to do, and they have answered "Nothing." What portent do the Churches of Scotland, looking towards the future, read into this terrible negation?

12

The Fishermen of the North East

Scotland, 1938

When we read in the press these days about the trials and tribulations of the Scottish fisherman, his demands for Government aid in the way of subsidies or foreign markets, the parlous condition of his boat and the amount he is in debt, some of us may wonder exactly what all the noise is about. After all, these men have their boats and the sea, and if prices may not be very good occasionally, still they should always be able to make some sort of living; in contradistinction, say, to an industrial area where when works are closed down employment for the mass of the workers is definitely not to be had. Moreover, in these comparatively sparsely populated areas of the north of Scotland, where the fishing is mostly carried on, there could not be the same distress as is found in a badly hit industrial area, for there is not only a healthier social environment but also the land, and the fisherman-crofter, once the common type, is still by no means unknown. In short, you can hardly expect the Government—or the ordinary citizen for that matter—to have a great deal of sympathy for fishermen, particularly in view of the pressing demands of the great primary industries and the problems of rearmament and international affairs.

Now to give some idea not only of the extent but of the tragedy of the error in this point of view, I may be forced to quote a few figures. But I shall try to be brief, though here the human side is so bound up with the economic that it would be impossible to convey anything of the hopes and fears of the people, of their struggles and happiness, without at least indicating the overriding factors that shaped their destiny and in due course produced so appalling a decline.

For I doubt if any scheduled or distressed area anywhere can show a comparable and, at the moment, so apparently hopeless a decline. I despair of trying to convey to the casual reader—for we are nearly all casual readers in such matters—the rich and fervent life that existed on that north-eastern coast a generation or two ago. If, for example, a visitor to Wick to-day, after discovering he did not require all his fingers to count Wick's own herring fleet, happened to look up the Statistical Account of Scotland for 1840, he would find the number of boats engaged in the summer herring fishing for that year neatly tabulated as follows: Native boats, 428; Strange boats, 337; total, 765. Granted, they were not very big boats, not normally exceeding about thirty feet, but each would have its crew of five, for the crews total 3828. But that was merely the fish-catching personnel. On shore there were over 4000 persons directly engaged in the industry. There were 91 curers, for example, 265 coopers, 2175 women, 1200 seamen in vessels exporting herring, not to mention carters and labourers and others. As the reverend gentleman who wrote the account at the time puts it, "No care was taken of the 10,000 young strangers of both sexes who were crowded together with the inhabitants within the narrow limits of Wick during the six weeks or so of the fishing." Altogether, reverend gentlemen were very disturbed about this increase in the wealth and personal freedom of their parishioners. The herring-fishing has "increased the population and augmented the rental of the parish, but whether it has added to the happiness and comfort of the people at large may well be questioned.... If it has increased the wealth it has also increased the wickedness of the district." But the same writer also contrives to say of the same people, "In particular, their minds are deeply imbued with suitable impressions of an overruling Providence governing all things according to the Divine will." Admittedly, it must have been a difficult situation for a shepherd of a well-trained flock, when in that short summer season anything up to 500 gallons of whisky a day, in the official phrase, "went into consumption." Not that it was all, so to speak, drunk off, or even then that the quantity per mouth would compare with the consumption of a stand at a fashionable racecourse. The curer would present a boat with seven gallons or so, and any member of the crew who did not feel equal to his whole share took part of it home with him. But after making all allowances, there must have been considerable and hectic goings-on amongst the 10,000 on the quays of Wick during these old fishing seasons!

But there we are talking of Wick, a large fishing port, with a decline in employment greater and apparently more irrevocable than in any shore industry comparable in magnitude. You may be able to turn workers of a declining primary or heavy industry into workers of what are called the secondary or light industries, but sea-fishing cannot be turned into anything else and knows only two categories: success or failure. If someone could hunt out the vital statistics for Wick to show, in particular, the number of families that have emigrated from that small town in the last generation, the figures, I am satisfied, would be astonishing.

Yet Wick is still a fishing port, with its seasons—if without its whisky! But what about the great number of creeks and harbours along the Moray Firth coasts, each fishing in its heyday anything up to two hundred boats, that have almost been completely wiped out? Grass-grown curing stations, gaping cooperages, sagging harbour walls, broken-down jetties, quay-walls undermined or ruinous, tell their own tale without any words. But if statistics are wanted, I may refer the curious to Peter F. Anson's *Fishing Boats and Fisher Folk of the East Coast of Scotland.* Ministers of the gospel are no longer afraid of the wickedness that triumphant fishings may bring to their flock. On the contrary, they hold prayer-meetings along the small creeks to-day, praying to all the Powers, temporal and spiritual, that the desolation may not become the abomination of desolation.

And having mentioned Mr Anson's name, perhaps as a writer and artist who knows so intimately and sympathetically the fishermen of our coasts, he may forgive me for referring to a matter that is personal but, to my way of thinking, so extremely illuminating. After years of exhaustive personal enquiry and study, involving not a little expense, into the whole subject of the sea-fisheries and fishermen of Britain, he at last completed what is *the* authoritative work on the subject, illustrated wherever necessary by line drawings expressive and accurate. We have no such printed work in our language. Yet publisher after publisher has refused the risk of printing it. We have not presumably even sufficient public libraries that would purchase a copy and so cover the cost of production. The student, anxious to know of the history of our British fisheries, has to go to a work in German.

Yet what a remarkable body of men sailed these northern and western seas throughout the last century! Courage and resource and daring were the common because the essential virtues. It is only within the lifetime of many men still living that decked boats came into use. The 1162 boats that fished out of Wick in 1862 would nearly all have been open or undecked boats. A fisherman, who has barely reached the allotted span, once gave me a remarkable picture of the herring fleet sailing out of a creek on the Caithness coast when he was a boy. Though the curing stations and cooperages are now in ruinous decay, about one hundred and fifty boats fished out of the creek during the summer seasons of his boyhood and indeed until he was a grown man. How lovely a sight from that river-mouth, from that small horse-shoe bay in the gaunt cliff-wall of Caithness, when the fleet, all under sail, left for the fishing grounds in the afternoon or early evening! And what hopes went with them! Not only from those they had left at home, but from the small army of curers and coopers and women gutters for whom good fortune in the catch meant employment and money. There was hardly a home in all that crofting hinterland but would be affected by the result. Fishing was not only an employment but a game, a thrill, and the first inland greeting in the morning was, "Any word of the boats to-day?"

They did not sail far afield in those early days, for the shoals of herring, undisturbed on the high seas by drifters and high-powered craft that may now go a hundred miles to meet them, came inshore in the way of nature, and when, say, a Lybster man heard that boats out of Scrabster had struck herring, he would know that in three days or so they would be off his own village—somewhere.

This fisherman told me that when the boats had taken their positions and shot their nets, there followed one of the most impressive things he had ever heard in this life—and heard not only in the boats themselves but from the land, for the boats were usually at no great distance from the shore. In the glimmer of the summer evening, one boat would "lift" the words of a psalm to one of the old tunes, and boat after boat would take it up, until the sea itself seemed to sway to the slow rhythm of the singing voices. He said it had a strange and deep effect on one. Not that that was the only music, he added, for often there would be someone with the bagpipes or other musical instrument to put something into the ear of the night!

Came the dawn, as the films say, and the hauling of the nets and the rush for berths, followed by an activity hectic enough for any cinematic lens. I can remember as a very small boy watching a woman-gutter to see if I could follow "how she did it" and being baffled. There they were, row after row of them, in stiff rustling oilskins, well-booted and shawled, silver-scaled and blood-flecked, with faces all alive; quick-voiced in retort or laughter, working, as we said, "like lightning." And all of them local women or girls, making their little bit while the going was good. Any visitor got a fry of herring from the generous skipper, whether a black-hooded widow from the hills or the friendly policeman from beside the church. Even though there were folk that were lucky and folk that decidedly were not! For, in the seaman's working philosophy, a generous hand never did a man any harm.

In those days, most of the fishermen also had crofts, though as time went on and decked boats came into use, there grew up a race of skippers who gave their whole attention to the sea, employing members of their own families and crofters or their sons as crews. The year was now divided up into fishing seasons. As May approached there was all the bustle and excitement of preparing for the West Coast fishing—tarring, painting, net mending and "barking," down to the laying in of a stock of ship's biscuits called "Barra biscuits"—beloved of the young, by whom, I fear, they were occasionally "raided." Then the day of departure, the rhythmic creak-creak of the halyards, the bellying of the great brown main-sails, and they were off! Down through the Caledonian Canal or north-about through the treacherous Pentland Firth, they took their gallant ways, scarcely forty feet in length, with no power beyond sail and oar, to fish from Stornoway or Castlebay, and for two months to take what was coming to them in profit or loss, calm or dangerous seas, in the Western Ocean. Back again for the summer fishing at home. And now the northeast coast drew Gaelic-speaking "hired men" from the West, for there were not sufficient local men to make up the crews. Not to forget the Peterhead and Fraserburgh season, when often a skipper would take his wife and young child or two with him, to house ashore. For the winter and spring months there were the white fishing and again some herring fishing.

But it is impossible in a short space to give any clear idea of the routh of warm life there was along all that north-east coast in the great days of the herring fishings, or to go into the reasons for its decline. The coming of the steam drifter, the mechanization of the industry, the withdrawal of curing from the small creeks to the large ports, the loss of foreign markets through political ineptitude, the growth of the fishing fleets of other nations helped in recent years by direct State aid or through a system of bounties and tariffs, while our fleet is left to struggle as it can, without any aid beyond a half-hearted effort at organization, based on restriction.

But it is a tragic tale, blind in its suffering, that has all but killed that glowing life, with its breed of great-hearted men and fine women.

13

'… and then Rebuild It'

Scots Magazine, 1939

In recent years we have had many books dealing with the economic ills and mental troubles of poor old Scotland. We know she is in a bad way; in fact, we know it so well, have scanned so many columns of figures, contrasted so many percentages, dealing with slums, unemployment, public health, housing, population, that, if not finally disheartened, at least we are wearied by so depressing a tale. Yet it would be a great pity if such a feeling were to turn us away from Dr Bowie's new book. *The Future of Scotland*. Indeed, if I had any power in such matters, I would strongly recommend this book to all social study circles for this winter.

For Dr Bowie, who is Principal of the School of Economics and Commerce in Dundee, handles statistics as the trained investigator should, and sets them forth free from all political or party bias. The word Socialism does not occur once, nor the word Toryism, and Nationalism he glances at only for a moment to state that manifestly the time is not yet. That does not mean he has not his own ideas on what requires to be done. His final section is, in fact, headed 'Summary and Proposals'. These proposals represent a planning of our economy based on ascertained facts and are in themselves, whether one agrees or not, suggestive and stimulating. His outlook is neither partial nor regional, but embraces Scotland as a whole. Far from being reassured, for example, by an increase in employment in Scotland due to armaments, Dr Bowie sees the inevitability of what is going to happen when the war is over—unless we begin the right kind of industry-building now; and he knows the right kind and suggests proved methods of setting about the business.

But before tackling any man's proposals (always debatable in our country), let us consider for a little how he treats his ascertained or statistical facts. The first section in the book is entitled, 'The Population of Scotland', and deals with census figures, 'the southward drift', emigration, sex and age distribution, birth and death rates, causes of decline in the birth-rate, the effects of a declining population; in short, it covers the whole field statistically and with clear regard to cause and effect. In the ten years to 1931 the population of Scotland declined by almost 40,000, while the population of England and Wales increased by over 2,000,000. The three factors governing population are births, deaths, and emigration. Now the birth-rate is higher than the death-rate in Scotland, though both are declining; and actually the excess of births over deaths in the given period was 352,000. Accordingly there must have been an emigration of 392,000 before a decline of 40,000 in the total could be recorded. The loss to Scotland by emigration over the ten years was 8 per cent of her population, while to England the loss by emigration was only 0.5 per cent. Board of Trade Returns show that the great mass went abroad, but 63,000 must have gone to Europe and England, and, we may conclude, mostly to England; some of them would be returning English, for there was a decline in the number of English in Scotland at the end of the ten years (though those of English birth in Scotland remain much more numerous than those of Irish and Welsh birth combined). Dr Bowie gives his reasons for this excessive emigration, and remarks, 'So emigration tends to take the young, the healthy, the enterprising, the courageous and the adaptable, precisely those people of whom Scotland to-day stands most in need. There is no scientific evidence that Scotland is over-populated, and still less evidence that emigration will cure her persistent unemployment.'

At this point the amateur investigator usually stops, but Dr Bowie goes on to a clear analysis of sex and age distribution, and fact follows fact until one sees that 'as the dwindling number of children grow up each successive age-group reveals a numerical decline, with the result that Scotland is gradually becoming a land of older people'. What is going to be the outcome over, say, the next hundred years? Here one can only give 'the logical conclusions to which existing trends point'. Dr Bowie quotes one eminent authority to this effect, '…if no new social agencies intervene to check declining fertility' then 'a period of rapid decline would set in after about thirty years. In this estimate the population would be 81 per cent of its present size fifty years from now, and only 19 per cent of its present size a hundred years from now'. True, that if is a small but potent word, yet it can be countered only by the intervention of 'new social agencies'. We cannot get past the fact that the decline in the birth-rate has reduced this generation's potential mothers. After 1931 emigration, for various reasons, almost ceased. 'But if there is even a modest recovery in overseas emigration and if the present migration to England continues, it is probable that Scotland's decline will be expedited'.

Let us glance for a moment at the Highlands. In 1801 they contained about one-fifth of Scotland's population; to-day, about one-twentieth. All the time emigration has been draining away the best stock at a tremendous rate. Since 1931 deaths exceed births. The population is ageing. The number of potential mothers falling. 'Unless heroic measures are taken, there is every indication that the Highlands will become the Sahara of Scotland'.

Does that sound alarmist? Well, how are we going to counter the facts? Dr Bowie does not go into the economic conditions of the Highlands to-day, but to those of us who have, who are aware, for example, of the enormous amount of state aid pumped into the Hebrides every week by way of pension and dole, his figures certainly make us think furiously. After all, St Kilda *was* evacuated. If there is not a livelihood in crofting-fishing for the average Hebridean head of a family under the existing economic dispensation—what's to be done about it? And if nothing is done?

But here I have merely been trying too compactly, to indicate the searching nature of Dr Bowie's inquiry into our population statistics. He does not leave the matter there but goes on to consider 'The quality of our people', and deals with school children, sickness, housing, nutrition, poverty, and our health services, producing facts as he goes along of a striking and often uncomfortable kind, with penetrating comment. When he comes to discuss Scotland's economic life the large issues of industry and unemployment are succinctly considered. This for many will be the vital section, because it concerns directly the future of our country.

Where fact and deduction are multiform and closely knit, it is presumptuous to try to give in a short space an adequate résumé. But here again two points may be singled out as illustration. Following the industrial revolution, Scotland specialised to an unparalleled degree in textiles and the heavy industries—coal, iron, steel and engineering. In recent years these industries have been permanently 'dethroned from their pre-eminent position, and our disproportionate dependence on them has been the root cause of our economic malaise'. Meantime, the new light industries—radio, motor car, aircraft, electrical engineering, synthetic products, and so on—'have become of fundamental importance in the modern world and offer the greatest possibilities of growth and development'; and it is just these industries that have failed to appear in any compensating measure in Scotland. Around London factories for these products have grown and are growing to an almost incredible extent, together with the necessary administrative services, 'including central and local government and commercial employment, and the satellite skilled services of banking, finance, insurance, accounting, scientific research, education, health, travel, and the defence services'.

Now we begin to get an understanding of Scotland's desperate record of unemployment, and we ask ourselves: But how could this have happened? Why should the London area have gone ahead in this way and the Glasgow area have failed? Dr Bowie discusses the matter, though here I feel he fails to isolate sufficiently the two unique factors: that London is the seat of government and the centre of finance. That London represents in itself a great market is only a comparative factor. Sweden, for example, with a population much less than London's has made enormous progress in the light electrical industries. And, after all, the Glasgow area, if we take it at a fourth or fifth of the London area, is in itself a great market, and if the light industries had developed there to a fourth or fifth of the extent they have developed around London, Scotland would have been relatively flourishing. Whether the Scots are inferior to the English in research, business method and workmanship may be debatable. That Scotland has neither a seat of government nor an integrated centre of finance is not debatable. Following on that are many supremely important psychological factors, for if nothing succeeds like success, nothing depresses like depression.

The second point I should like to mention is Dr Bowie's treatment of the Special Areas and the value of such trading estates as the one at North Hillington. To many readers this will be new matter, and Dr Bowie's inclusive view is constructive. Again the difference between Scotland and England is made clear. 'Thus in Scotland, as in no other equivalent area in England, the Special Area legislation has pooled industrial development in a small area in the West, and has doubled the difficulties under which other and now more depressed areas suffer.'

But from analysis we must pass with Dr Bowie to his constructive proposals, and here space precludes my even attempting a fair summary. But roughly Dr Bowie's idea is that we should go in for what has been called Planning, a Planned Economy. What has been attempted at North Hillington should be attempted all over. For this purpose we should not only have the necessary research and other bodies working things out, but over all a Commission with powers to apply the findings. Every issue as it arose, even to the transference of a community from a permanently derelict area, would be realistically and sympathetically dealt with.

And just here the argument starts! Not that the argument would be against Planning as such—therein lies the intrinsic value of Dr Bowie's research—for Planning has become essential to socialist and capitalist alike, while for the nationalist (who may be either) the need for building up his country is the motive power of his creed.

The trouble is that in Scotland we have historic reason to smile at the idea of any London-appointed Commission doing anything of real constructive value. We have been disillusioned too often. Granted that a perfectly constituted Commission, permanently in session, with adequate finance, could accomplish much; but your Commission in that case would be tantamount to a government, though of rather an autocratic type, because it would not be directly responsible to the people of the country in which it would be operating. Let it be responsible to the people concerned through the usual democratic channels and you have government. Without going outside our democratic conception of a state, it is difficult to see the matter in any other light. Dr Bowie seems to think it would be easier to get such a Commission than to get a Government. I wonder! After all, there is a profound psychological impulse behind the desire to govern your life in your own way; there is none in the idea of getting a Commission to do it for you. Would it be going too far to suggest that most of the individual work that has been done in recent years in examining Scottish conditions (of which the present book is an excellent example) has been a direct result of the re-awakened interest in self-government? Again, where special commissions have studied and worked and produced recommendations, what has usually happened? Little or nothing. Take one of the most fruitful—the recent inquiry into the Highlands. Dr Bowie has not dealt with the economic conditions of the Highlands, with the great industry of the sea-fisheries and the peculiar conditions of the crofting areas (how would his large 'factory' farm apply here?). But I would merely suggest that the annual grant of £65,000 for five years *spread over all the purposes stated is* just absurd. The gillie's tip on a larger scale. If even the government had said, 'We will plan the lobster fisheries, from lobster pond to transport and marketing', one would at least have seen something constructive being attempted. But that is just the sort of thing that never happens. Or take, again, the Scottish National Development Council, which in its minor way is not unlike a permanent Commission. What's happening to it now? What is it likely to do with regard to planning and bringing into being new industries for Scotland now and in the critical future? The last I heard of it was that its quarterly magazine, *Scotland,* which was devoted in some measure to that very research into economic conditions which Dr Bowie deems so fundamental, has ceased publication. In a desire to avoid controversy, we are liable to plan logical structures on a wishful basis. And the London Treasury doesn't mind—until we beg for cash to build somewhere other than in the air.

There is one direct criticism I should like to make because I think it is fundamental. It has become a commonplace to condemn the Scot for being an individualist, unable to combine in co-operative effort. Dr Bowie refers to this strongly more than once. Many go the length of saying that Scotland's present desperate condition is due almost entirely to this destructive flaw in our characters, and, as it is innate, we need not look for any material improvement in our condition.

I discussed this matter at some length in a recent issue of this magazine. Here let me conclude with a few observations upon it. Dr Bowie mentions the Scots who go south and become 'heids o' depairtments'. But a man who satisfies his ambition by departmental work, requiring for perfect functioning a high degree of co-ordination and co-operation, is manifestly not the incorrigible individualist. If the departments were available in his own country, presumably he would function in them with the same skill. The machinery for initiating and co-ordinating constructive effort in Scotland, backed by the necessary finance, does not exist. It would have to be a national machinery, directly answerable to the Scottish taxpayer whose money it would use. Any other kind of machinery would be in the nature of an insecure makeshift, that would be suspended whenever a 'state of emergency' arose—that is, at the very time (the present moment, for example) when it would be supremely important that it should be working and planning full time over against the inevitable depression that would swamp our heavy industries when the emergency had passed.

One final word. A study of the Scottish scene from the early clan days of highly-developed communal effort to the institutions Scotland has tended to produce in the course of her history as a nation shows clearly that the democratic co-operative structure was natural to her from an early age. It has been said more than once that the Scottish Church system of government, with its kirk sessions and assemblies, may have given more than a few hints to the founders of the USSR! However that may be, I have the odd conviction that if a Government, based on democracy and co-operation, had been functioning in Scotland in recent decades Dr Bowie would now probably himself be the head of a department concerned with research necessary to the launching of what would be to us the usual Quinquennial Plan.

14

Scotland Moves

Scots Magazine, 1943

In the years before the war, I used to get an occasional letter from students in Continental universities asking questions about Scotland, which they wished to make the subject of a thesis for some diploma or other. Was there a distinct Scottish spirit, a true national ethos, and if so where could its best expression to-day be found? Was there a real difference between Highland and Lowland? And so on. Some of the questions were surprisingly searching, and I was hard put to it to give a reasonably clear answer.

To-day I have a letter from an old friend whose countrymen are not directly involved in this war, asking me if Scotland publishes a magazine which is concerned with real poetry, and whether extracts from a long poem, written by one of his friends and just published in America, might appeal to the editor of such a magazine and be printed in the usual way at the usual rates. The subject matter of the poem has an historic connection with Scotland.

Or, again, here is a professional crowd doing a 'short' for the films; 'the subject matter has a Scottish background, and the singing of a Gaelic chorus and of a psalm has already been recorded. Incidental music has now to be written for the film, and its idiom must clearly be Scottish in order to achieve a harmonious total effect. Could the name of a Scottish composer, who might successfully undertake the task, be given?'

But most of us are aware of this interest in Scottish life on its political or economic side. As a people we are not greatly concerned about the arts. An artist or writer has still to go to London in order that he may be near what is called 'the centre of things', in other words that he may get sufficient bread and butter to keep him alive while finding an outlet for his talent or genius. Yet even here one or two careless spirits have stuck to their native heath and appear to be going on as well as could be expected. It may be a far cry to an Edinburgh of brilliance and creative force, to such an Edinburgh as in some measure the world did once upon a time know, but in quite recent days I have heard a poached salmon being wagered against a jug of beer that Edinburgh will yet attain her truly golden age—even though time may compel the wager to be paid in another place.

However, on the practical side we are all happily aware not only of the interest that has been aroused in Scottish affairs but of the sheer amount of hard work that has already been done. To anyone who has not been closely following these developments, it might be difficult to give in a word or two a fair summary of the position. For there is more in it than just what has been done either in actual accomplishment or in planning, in the sense that the whole mental approach has altered. For example, before the war, the Government recognised that something had to be done for the Highlands or they would revert to an uninhabited wilderness. So, taking their courage in their hands, those in London who control our destinies decided that nothing less than £65,000 a year for five years would meet the dreadful necessity.

Just then the war broke out, so the Government at once withdrew their munificent offer. The country could not afford so huge a sum in constructive work now that a devastating war was upon us.

Yet in recent months, we have all been following the smooth passage of the Secretary of State's Hydro-Electric Bill, wherein an expenditure of £3,000,000 is contemplated on one single aspect of Highland reconstruction, namely, the harnessing of water power.

But the change is even greater than the figures might indicate, for the Government's approach is not based on charity or dole but on what we call a real business proposition. In other words, the hydro-electric scheme is going to pay for itself. This tapping of Highland water power is not merely a something that will benefit the Highlands but a constructive act that will enrich the whole country.

This change in the mental weather is what the Highlands have needed for generations. Nothing in the long run is so deadly to a people as charity or the dole, far more deadly than to an individual who can at any moment break his fetters and clear out.

And that this new approach was just what was needed can be proved fairly simply by considering the fate of Highlanders, over the distressful generations, who were burned out of their homes and shipped to Canada, or who in despair or the name of fortune voluntarily emigrated. Names like Fraser or Mackenzie wander as mighty rivers across a continent. The defeatism bred of a paralysing history is forgotten, and an energy and resource are released that astonish the critics, and that in fact still contrive to astonish the world in the deeds of the Highland Division.

This is not said in boastfulness—that dubious form of self-expression which can more usefully be left to the psychoanalysts. Its immense importance to us lies in just this—that it should help us to assess the true potential of any new constructive measures at home. It should let us see the kind of constructive effort that is needed. By it we can recognise that the approach to the problem of harnessing Highland hydro-electric power is sound, simply because it presents the opportunity for the exercise of energy and resource at home.

There are critics who say that there are flaws in the plan, even dangers, that everything in the electric garden is not lovely. No doubt. But I have never yet had anything to do with a garden but it required a fair amount of work to keep it even presentable. But, given the garden, surely it's a poor spirit that complains before the work is started.

I have mentioned the hydro-electric scheme simply because it is perhaps the first evidence of the coming fruit. But a great deal of exploratory work is also being accomplished in other realms of Scottish life, from herring fishing to hill sheep-farming, from hospitals and rehabilitation to the inauguration of planning on a regional scale. We have had the report by the Forestry Commission, for example, duly debated in Parliament. But the majority of Scots want a separate Forestry authority for Scotland. And those who have been most vocal or active in this demand are not Nationalist or Socialists, but Tories of the House of Lords. In other words, the need for such a separate authority has become so obvious that it has cut across all party lines. It is seen to be absurd that a Forestry Commission, overwhelmingly English and with headquarters in London, should be governing the destinies of sheep farmers and forestry concerns in the Highlands. If we have a separate Department of Agriculture in St Andrew's House surely it is but commonsense that a Forestry department should also be there, so that both could combine in a long term policy which would ensure the minimum of hardship and the maximum of gain for the country as a whole. The point becomes still more obvious when we realise that the greater part of the planted acreage administered by the Forestry Commission is already in Scotland.

But having thus indicated the kind of concentration that is now taking place by Scotsmen on Scottish affairs, perhaps we need not go on giving instances. As the reports of the Secretary of State's Committees continue to appear we shall have plenty to think about—and no doubt to quarrel over. Out of all this ferment, two points may call for special attention.

First, there is the feeling—though not now so strong as it was some time ago—that all this concern with post-war conditions is in some degree unreal and in some degree dangerous because it may distract us from our main purpose of winning the war. Moreover, how can those of us who are too old to fight be trusted with the work of recreating an economy for the lads who are fighting and who are necessarily denied any criticism of our labours? For it is they who will have to work the schemes and ensure the future generations.

Let it be clear that this feeling is expressed not by the soldiers themselves, but by those of us at home who prefer to remain armchair critics of the conduct of the war and who must not be distracted from this high task by doing a spot of useful constructive labour. Take, as an instance, the Beveridge Report. Now we do know that this Report had an enormous interest for the soldiers in Libya. It aroused such enthusiasm that apparently some kind of political action had to be taken. Anyway, I think it can be safely said that the soldier felt that Sir William Beveridge was putting up a real fight for him on the home front. The value of that Report as world propaganda for our country must have been immense. If Britain can think like this, at such a time, then plainly she is not the devitalised country some nations thought she was!

Or take our Highland hydro-electric scheme. The constructional period will give work to 10,000 men for ten years. Well, we know what happened after the last war. Is there any soldier in the Highland Division who will feel less happy because a Secretary of State for Scotland is trying *now* to make fairly certain that there will be a job for him when he comes home?

If no work of this kind were being done by those of us who can fight in no other way, would not the soldier indeed have reason to condemn us as betrayers of what he has left in our charge? That is the real question which we have to answer.

The second point is this, and we have got to contemplate it with as little prejudice as possible. Such research and constructional work, through advisory councils and committees, through direct measures by our Secretary of State, and in other ways, is being done by Scotsmen in Scotland. For the first time in centuries the feeling is growing upon us that we can do things for ourselves. More than that, we are beginning to realise that we cannot expect others to do them for us; and perhaps this is the greater gain, because it holds more hope for Scotland's future.

15

Belief in Ourselves

Scots Magazine, 1945

Unless you could get a lift from someone with petrol coupons, a permit to show to soldiers at a barrier, the assurance of a resting-place that was officially blameless, travelling in some of the most attractive areas of the Highlands was forbidden even to those of us who had homes in the Highlands.

Now that we can freely breathe the mountain air again, and look at places, and even ask friendly questions about what's going on without raising the worst kind of suspicion, we are prepared to leave definitions of the blessed word freedom to the pundits. If we are wise, we even decide on the kind of society and its ordering that we are not going to have. Truly there are certain things that no good man gives up but with his life. Freedom is a noble thing, said the old poet, and we salute him across the whole landscape and history of Scotland. In our beginning was the word.

So the Highlands burst once more upon the astonished eyes. The idea that tourist traffic must be *encouraged* seems a colossal joke. Given a society with the necessities of life reasonably provided, a pocket full of holidays and pay, and we need have no fantastic worry about the places that like to be visited. They'll be visited all right.

But there remains that worry about the decent ordering of a basic economic life in the Highlands: and what I should like to do here is mention one aspect of it. It is the simplest matter in the world to set down on paper a full scheme for Highland regeneration. We all know the ingredients by this time as we know the words of an old song: crofting, hill sheep-farming, sea fisheries, hydro-electric development, afforestation, appropriate light industries, transport, and so on. But there is one thing that is always missing, one all-important matter which the paper economists forget, and that is the general lack of belief among the Highland people themselves in the future of their own land as a place where life could be lived interestingly and well.

Let me put it like this. Assuming you met a hundred Highland lads newly demobilised from the distinguished 51st Division, and said to them: 'We have word from Canada that there are excellent jobs awaiting you all over there', would they believe you? You know they would, to a man. They might or might not want to go to Canada, but they would believe you. Assuming, however, you said to them that the place was the Highlands, would there be the same response, the same automatic belief? There wouldn't. Instead you would see a sarcastic glimmer in their eye, a wonder what the leg-pull was about. First-class jobs in the Highlands! A few, who really love the Highlands, might not in the circumstances consider the joke as in the best taste. Seriously, and before committing themselves, they would then ask about the Canadian jobs, for one hopes to live with reasonable security outside the fighting line.

Now it would be no good going on to point out to these lads the real and potential wealth of the Highlands. It would be just talk. They knew what they knew, and that would be that. For what would be fundamentally lacking would be not fact, but belief. They could go to Canada, take land, blast the trees off it and make it fertile, build dams and factories, pioneer and create, as their folk had done before them (and in a way that was never better done), but to be asked to use the same creative energy at home with the certainty of at least as good a result or livelihood—no, impossible. No one did that sort of thing or believed it ever could be done in the old decaying homeland. The place is finished. It's no use making the effort. The very thought of it makes a fellow tired.

Let me look at it another way. Some time ago I had occasion to criticise a certain official report on our herring industry. I cannot go into the matter here, but roughly let it be said that, whereas the English herring fleets are run by shore syndicates, the Scottish boats are owned on the whole by the fishermen themselves and run on a co-partnership or share basis. Now, as we know, the small individually-owned business is carrying on a losing fight against the multiple concern. Before the war the Scottish boats were badly in debt, and their future looked very black. The individual hasn't the resources of the syndicate when it comes to tiding over a difficult time. The syndicate can hang on until the individual is sunk—and then take over his business or his boat.

But, it seemed to me, it would not be a very difficult bit of organising for all the individually-owned Scottish boats to group themselves into a League or Co-operative, with central resources from levies that would enable them to meet the English syndicates on their own level, and in fact beat them at their own game, for they would then have a greater concentration of shore capital and resources (they have more boats), and also could divide the profit on capital among themselves in any form they liked.

I am told that what I wrote was considered by our fishermen in one or two places. But they shook their heads. They just did not believe the thing could be done. Impossible.

But it has been done in other countries. And sea-fishing will not forever know the artificial restrictions of war-time, the reduced fleets, the certain market, the high prices. Yet there is little use pointing out these facts and drawing inevitable conclusions. Belief is lacking. The thing cannot be done in Scotland. In Norway, South Africa, the Soviet Union—yes, but that's different!

Let me consider a refreshing instance of where on a small scale a co-operative effort among a group of crofters has been successful. After the last war, the Board of Agriculture helped ex-servicemen who were crofters to combine in the possession of hill sheep-farms. Prices for sheep were very high at the time, and unfortunately the many sheep clubs thus formed had to take over from the Board at what in too many instances—especially on the West Coast—proved a crippling figure. I need not go into all that here, nor applaud the fine intentions of the Board (as the Department of Agriculture still continues to be called in our remoter places). This particular club which I visited in Caithness last week had not only weathered the storm of ever-declining prices in the inter-war years, but had at last successfully cleared off their capital indebtedness to the Board of several thousand pounds. There are twenty-six crofters in the club, and they now are the sole owners of a sheep stock of some 1500 head, managed by three shepherds. Their profit last year, after expenses of every kind were paid, amounted to £1040. In short, each crofter received £40 as his share. And, over and above, he has behind him his capital share of the stock which at current prices is a tidy sum. However you look at it, not a discouraging result for communal or co-operative effort!

I was at the sheep-clipping where all the club members turn out to give a hand. It was a pleasant gathering, with talk going strong on politics, land reclamation, and all the topics of the day, while small boys were tripping over the fleeces they bore away to those who rolled and packed them. It was a scene reminiscent of an older Highland economy, when neighbours assisted one another not only at clipping, but at peat-cutting and harvest, and indeed on any occasion when necessity called for a helping hand. The Highlands were not unused to a common or co-operative effort, out of which, in fact, the warmth of life came, with the songs, the jokes and the ceilidhs. They had belief in life in those days, and in what they could do for themselves.

To see the shepherds organising and carrying through the clipping, their ability and friendliness with everyone, to partake of their wives' hospitality, to note the fiddle hanging on the wall and to know of the bagpipes in their box, was to be assured of what yet may be accomplished on a wider scale and in many ways. I had only to remember the time when there was no club farm here. Had anyone said then that crofters' sheep would one day have the run of grouse moor and deer forest, organised on a club basis and managed by three shepherds, who would have believed him?

It took a Government Department to set it going. Well, why not? What is a Department for if not to assist enterprise which will increase the wealth of the country? The Department gave them the start, helped men who had fought for their country to do something in peace time for themselves. And so helped, the men went ahead, paid back the Department, and are now reaping the reward of their belief in what could be done in their own glen, on their own moors.

And so much more requires to be done even on these moors. Bracken has invaded the green river flats—the fertile land that could grow grass for silage and winter feed. Wintering the hoggs last year cost a pound per head. The hill drains need opening. And beyond sheep there are the new—and very old—thoughts about breeds of hardy cattle. In the old days it was an economy of cattle and sheep. A tremendous amount of research has been—and is being—done into all this. We have recently had a Report on hill sheep-farming by an independent committee. We are beginning to see what could be accomplished; and what undoubtedly will be, if only among ourselves we believed in it and went at it as we undoubtedly would—in Canada.

In all this there is one thing that particularly interests me, and that is that I should like to see the new energy and impetus provided by Highlanders themselves, by those who derive from the old traditions, the old race, so that what was distinctive and fine in our culture, our ways of life and behaviour, might continue. But vital statistics show that this will have to be done soon or it will be too late. Emigration is a remorseless way of getting rid of the best. And a dwindling population adds ever new ruins to the old ruins in the glens.

16

New Golden Age for Scottish Letters

Daily Record, 1930

Would I call it a Renaissance? Either that, or an Awakening. The Scottish Awakening would be rather an amusing description, and even an arresting one to those countries that have come to think that the Scotsman never sleeps.

To suggest that a Prime Minister is likely to awake, or an Archbishop to yawn at the devotions, or a Mr Maxton to turn in his sleep (other than uneasily) might make the world wonder.

But as it is the obvious desire of the new writers (despite their critics) not to covet publicity wantonly, I certainly would be inclined to vote for 'Renaissance'. To most of us it happily means nothing. But to the rest it raises the classic challenge.

Let the word connote a rebirth of letters, of the arts. But really it stands for much more than that to us.

We at once think of something like the Italian Renaissance, that is a period where we now are not only in at the birth but also, as it were, at the death.

In this way the Scottish effort invites amusing but irrelevant ridicule. We expect it to take off its heady dram without a cough, when in the normal way it should be gurgling over its mother's milk. A child is never ridiculous. But its grown-up critics nearly always are – even when they're friendly.

Though that doesn't mean that the critic in your columns recently who suggested that this hailing of every new Scottish writer as a genius, is bad for him and worse for Scottish letters, is in any better case. He is taking his own wisdom altogether too seriously.

And it is not much in the way of satire to imply that a 'genius' is not a genius. To flatter a writer unduly always adds to our gaiety, even when, if the writer is sensitive, it is in bad taste.

There is always some excitement in a true enthusiasm. But not every writer who is called a genius tries to dress accordingly. So the critic may calm himself.

In fact one or two of our finest young writers have told me that they dislike the label intensely!

It is possibly a handicap in the sense that it may make them blush and gnash their teeth. But we need not agree with them, for in the process of gnashing their teeth there is always the sporting chance of cutting one or two new ones.

And, anyway, it is a desperately beguiling handicap. It worries and annoys— and drives. It may help those who have it in them to out with it. Birth is a notoriously painful process. And not every critic is a twilight sleep.

But apart from that, wherefore the label Renaissance? Firstly, because of the distinctive work done these last few years, and, secondly (and more importantly), because of the existence of an immense national reserve awaiting the act of creation. As to the writers who have so far distinguished themselves, I say nothing here.

If they aren't all geniuses, neither are the writers of any country at any time, barring the odd one. Nor is a renaissance exclusively concerned with genius in any case. Not that I subscribe to the idea that genius will out willy nilly.

There's quite a lot in the 'mute inglorious Milton' – particularly when he has not merely been forcibly inhibited but at the same time directed to an outlet that can never let him out. Renaissance is really concerned with the bringing to birth once more of a culture, in this particular case a Scottish culture, on a national scale.

If, however, we had not this immense reserve, which cannot be properly worked by anyone but a Scot, the whole idea would be absurd. As it happens, we have. And on a truly magnificent scale.

Whether we like it or not, our ancestors spoke Gaelic for many more centuries than they spoke English. How they came by it we may not know, even if there are those who are prepared to plump for the Garden of Eden.

But we do know how they came by English; they acquired it. That doesn't mean that we must all start writing in Gaelic at once.

Even our critics' logic can be occasionally amusing in this respect. But it does mean that we should gain some knowledge of a culture which was in its most perfect flower centuries before even the beginnings of English Literature.

Why? Simply because we derive from it, and all art starts from self-knowledge in its profounder aspects. In a more restricted way we derive also from that powerful variant of the English tongue called Scots, the ballads and the Makars.

We need not consider here how it came about that we grew rather self-conscious of both. All that need concern us is that we did, but that we are now better able to assess not merely the value of what we discarded, but also the value of what we tried to put in its place.

And once the Scot has got his sense of proportion again, his reborn pride in his heritage will be a driving force that will know no early or timid or baffled exhaustion. Why is it that since Scott there have been so many Scotsmen of promise, men who have started off brilliantly but who have weakly and unaccountably petered out?

I believe it is simply because they had no faith in, were not profoundly conscious of, their life-giving roots.

But the world knows the Scot for a fighter. And once this fight is properly joined I can hardly think of his giving in easily.

In a word, I cannot see how we are to avoid, even if we would, a new age, possibly a golden age, in Scottish letters.

But though an individual genius may emerge in a day, a culture is not born in one. This means a horrid process of 'gradualism'? Not at all.

In the historic sweep, for a big movement to be born and flower in half a century is near enough the instantaneous not to matter.

17

The Scottish Renascence

Scots Magazine, 1933

> In the following essay, Neil Gunn, using a pseudonym, replied to an article by Gordon Leslie Rayne, which had appeared in the previous issue of *The Scots Magazine*, entitled This Scottish Tongue: the Renascence and the Vernacular'.

In his article in your last issue on 'The Renascence and the Vernacular', Mr Gordon Leslie Rayne has the disarming suavity of one who would present his keenest barb sheathed in cotton wool before shoving it home by inadvertence. The operation is courteous, if more than a trifle obscured. Indeed through the final 'woolliness' I find it difficult to assess what exactly has taken place, or even, with clearness, what it is that Mr Rayne designed should take place, for he is all for encouraging every man, such as he is.

Broadly, however, his charge would appear to be that there are those who proclaim a Scottish Renascence when in reality there is no such thing. Or, as he puts it himself, he has been 'slightly puzzled by the vociferous heralds of a Scottish Renascence which somehow I seem to have missed,' and then attempts to show that what he has missed can hardly be held to have existence in fact.

Now this is the true national game, for it allows the ironic off-taking of our neighbours without which no Scot among us ever really feels properly bedded or safe. We rise to this lure almost before it lands, and leave our surface chuckles to ring the inane. Observe, for example, that Mr Rayne uses the words 'vociferous heralds'. Others on the same quest have used similar lures. There has thus been created the impression of a host of clamant individuals (little higher than the angels) heralding the miraculous rebirth in letters of Scotland's spirit. It sounds good fun straight away. It ensures for Mr Rayne his 'deep chuckle' before he has right started, thus aligning his technique with that of 'the genius of Sir Harry Lauder'. Sense and sanity are immediately enthroned upon that guid conceit which is going to have moderation in all else, and particularly in everyone else (leaving the Lord to appraise exceptionally 'me and mine'). Yet all we have to do to destroy the good old game in this particular instance is to ask Mr Rayne to produce his 'vociferous heralds'. It is as simple as that. Here is a book, for instance called *Scotland in Quest of Her Youth,* in which this very matter is touched upon by half a dozen of our known younger writers (Catherine Carswell, Naomi Mitcheson, James Bridie, George Blake, Eric Linklater, Neil Gunn). They are not only not vociferous heralds, but on the contrary severe critics of what has been accomplished, using an irony ruthless enough to indicate that very spirit they seek. Among the other younger Scottish writers of note, where are the 'vociferous heralds'? I have studied this modern 'Movement' as closely, I hope, as Mr Rayne, and I can think of only one writer to whom this appellation might be attached (and then only with a certain significance), and that writer is Mr C M Grieve. Those who have followed the early work of the Movement will understand the reason for this, but it need not detain us here, for my purpose may be served by asking Mr Rayne whether out of those recent generations of writers with whom he has been in touch there is one he can place against Hugh MacDiarmid (Mr C M Grieve) as a poet? There is none (surely none amongst those names he has mentioned), and I presume he must allow it. And poetry is the very flower of literature.

Now if I have dealt with this epithet of Mr Rayne's at undue length, it is because the whole attitude of mind in and behind it is very revealing. Indeed, it is the analysing of this attitude of mind that would probably be the swiftest and surest way of arriving at the heart of our quest. If we can show that the attitude to literature in its Scottish expression by what we may call the renascent writers is radically different from that shown by Mr Rayne's previous generations, then at once we have established a spiritual distinction. If the kailyairders were sentimental and deliquescent, and the new men are vital and life-giving, the change amounts to renascence or rebirth. Quintessentially it is not a matter of whether we are producing great writers so much as whether we are producing writers quick with this new validity or vitality. That is the real issue.

For manifestly it would be a useless dogmatic game to go on assessing one writer against another. Time is needed, apparently, to give the perspective that permits Shakespeare a higher place than Ben Jonson (to how deep an astonishment on the part of rare Ben—and of his friends!). Furthermore, if there is a Renascence, then clearly it has had very little time to get over the birth pangs; a very short time compared with, say, the reign of Robertson Nicoll (to cite one of Mr Rayne's 'mighty men'). Altogether let it be emphasised that renascence does not necessarily imply or demand the emergence of one or more great figures (though it nearly always coincides with this emergence), but rather a reawakening or rebirth of spirit amongst many people, ultimately discernible even in the minor social manifestations of a whole people.

I am tempted, however, to pause over that name, Robertson Nicoll, and to place against it one of our critics of to-day, who has shown concern with the

Renascence and is himself one of its significant figures, Edwin Muir. As critics, they have both been concerned with assessing literature, and however we may dispute their individual merits, I maintain that their attitude, their approach, their criteria or standards of judgement, exhibit a fundamental difference or divergence. This may be difficult to define in a sentence without seeming unfair, but, that granted, it might be said that Nicoll was concerned voluminously in his journalistic manner with what appealed to his personal idiosyncrasies, against a given local religious background, whereas Muir is concerned with the isolation of pure or permanent values by applying literary standards of a high, exacting kind. The most cursory study of Muir's work will show the plane of his debate and its remoteness from Robertson Nicoll's. I am not here concerned with personal gifts or abilities, but merely with indicating this difference or divergence, because appreciation of it is essential before what underlies any renascence claim can possibly be apprehended.

Let us take another example. 'The genius of Sir Harry Lauder,' writes Mr Rayne, 'is part and parcel of the kailyaird tradition, and since then our younger people have lost the gift of eliciting the deep chuckle and provoking the postponed, but persisting, grin of inner merriment. They are so desperately sober-sided. …' When Sir Harry tells his 'best one' about a Scotsman's meanness, and has the added joke of making money out of the transaction, the young renascent Scots have their chuckle all right, and, let Mr Rayne be assured, the grin of merriment persists. True, it is merriment with a difference, anything but sober-sided, positively Rabelaisian in its sweep, and any day it may burst out. Much as George Douglas Brown burst out, though I observe that Mr Rayne does not include that name amongst his mighty.

And so one could go on. Poetry I have already mentioned. In this Magazine there is verse (by William Soutar, for example), which has all the characteristics of the renascence temper, and is as different from the Magazine verse of a former generation as a divining rod from a Lauder crook. In fiction one could make, perhaps, the clearest claim of all.

Mr Rayne perceives there is something in all this, for he says the 'revolt' from the standards and ideals of the past 'is not peculiarly Scottish, it is essentially modern and current throughout Europe.' Yet further on he tries to ridicule the revolting Scot for *harking back* to Dunbar's pedantic tongue! Nor is our confusion clarified by his exclusive reference to tongue. He should know that the harking back to Dunbar is professedly not a harking back for language so much as a harking back for greatness. Dunbar is great in breadth, in variety and ingenuity, in largeness of conception and utterance, after the fashion that Chaucer before and Shakespeare after him were great. It is this lost greatness that the renascent Scot would strive to see restored, recognising that its manifestation in a nation at any time is due not so much to the odd appearance of an individual genius (generally forced to dissipate his best energies in rebellion), as to the existence within the nation itself of that aptitude for greatness out of which genius naturally flowers.

Finally, that the development of the Scottish nationality 'has nothing whatever to do with the continuance of the Scottish vernacular', may be correct. Scottish nationality may have nothing to do with the Gaelic tongue and literature. Having at last acquired English, it may be able to dispense with all history and tradition; it may indeed develop all the better for the lack of roots of any sort. Something of this parasitic conception of Scotland is common enough. All that can definitely be said is that the greatest poetry produced in Scotland since Dunbar has been in the Scottish tongue, that our only poetry to-day of European importance is being written in that tongue, and that, with all due deference to Mr Rayne, great poetry in whatever tongue makes a nation neither ridiculous nor ludicrous. For the rest, it would appear that Scotsmen have the chameleon-like quality of 'adaptability to the habits, the thoughts, and the speech of other nations'. Yet, adds Mr Rayne, our nationality is irrevocably bound up 'with the preservation of qualities and gifts of which the glorious company of the self-styled revivalists have yet to learn and think'.

If only Mr Rayne had helped us by explaining when his chameleon is not a chameleon and how! Unless, of course, all the 'qualities and gifts' had already been summed up by him in our genius for music-hall comedy, complete with deep chuckle and grin of merriment (continuing).

18

Literature: Class or National

Outlook, 1936

Though I happen to agree with much that Mr Lennox Kerr wrote under the above heading in your last issue, I must say that I feel he failed completely to make out his 'case against the claim that literature is national in origin'. In fact, in his provocative article he does not discuss the origins of literature at all, and his reply to the PEN's 'Literature, though national in origin, knows no frontiers and should be a common currency between nations ...' takes the evasive form of a discussion of class differences within existing political organisations.

The simple truth of the matter seems to be that literature is national in origin and has found its subject-matter or drama precisely in those class differences and other distinctions or inequalities which together make up the life of a nation. That such has been the case may—or may not—be unfortunate. That it is a fact is surely unquestionable. If we regard poetry as literature's highest expression, then literature still remains a national affair, for to this day great poetry does not bear translation from its own tongue into any other. Even in a country like Scotland, which has been doing its best, or worst, with English for some centuries, we are forced to recognise that the poetry, which has achieved more than a national reputation has been written in Scots.

And it may be interesting for Mr Kerr to reflect further that what we consider in Scotland our finest literature is largely an expression of the people, whether of yesterday in the *Scots Quair* of Lewis Grassic Gibbon, or the day before in Burns or Mary Macleod, or earlier in the Ballads, or earlier still in the ceilidh-house tales and poems; the expression of a folk who together make a unique nation. Burns is as well known in the Highlands as in the Lowlands. A Skyeman assures me that a generation ago he was the only poet, other than the Gaelic bards, known—and loved—in the Island. I can myself vouch for the far north. And decidedly the best of Burns is not a poetry produced to pander to the tastes, social or possessive, of those in power, any more than were the satires of the northern bards. It is not a mere accident that made *Sunset Song* so significant and stirring as literature compared with the English novels of Leslie Mitchell. In both his English and his Scots novels, Mitchell was always for the people, for the classless folk. No one hated more bitterly the social inequalities and tragedies resulting from the present organisation of society. But Mitchell had to come back to his own country, his own people, before what moved him so deeply received in profoundest expression. In the absence of any evidence to the contrary, that is what we have got to accept; and that is what, I take it, is implied by 'national origin' in the PEN declaration, or, if one likes, by the 'culture pattern' of our modern anthropologists. The culture pattern is susceptible of change, of course. What Mr Kerr has really done in his article is to indicate the form such a change may or should take.

Yet at this point I again feel that Mr Kerr evades the real issue by an attempt to 'escape' from it, like his middle-class artist, into a realm of political theory where literature's individuality is sunk in the major dictum, 'all art is propaganda'. I hope he will not misunderstand me if I say that this dictum is becoming intellectually fashionable, particularly amongst those—mostly *bourgeois*—who consider themselves as political rebels deriving from Lenin. Not nationalism but internationalism is their phrase. Not merely the stevedores of Glasgow and the stevedores of London (to whom Mr Kerr refers), but also the stevedores of Hamburg and Jibuti and Singapore and Venice. The culture change can be brought about only by the working classes of all nations making common cause against the capitalists of all nations. This is the sort of facile conception of direct action that may well be subversive of the very idea it carries. However, as it is possible to theorise endlessly, let us be realist or concrete; let us choose two cases: one, where such an economic change has taken place as realises more or less the classless order or working-class order of society desired by Mr Kerr; and, two, a country where a literary renaissance has actually resulted from a national rebirth. Let us take Russia and Ireland.

Now the first outstanding fact about Russian Communism is that it was built on a national basis. Lenin manifestly did not make it a *working* maxim that it would be impossible to get the stevedores of Archangel into a classless State without first of all getting the stevedores of Glasgow, London, etc, to link up with them in a revolutionary struggle. Although Russia was overwhelmingly peasant, Lenin did not approach the crofters of Wester Ross before collaring the land of Russia for the Soviet Republics. The social difference between a Russian landowner and the slave who bore the weals of his knout was vastly greater than the difference between Mr Kerr's Duke and his Communist MP in modern Scotland. But such differences did not deter Lenin: on the contrary, they spurred him on all the more strongly to realise his classless society in that place where he could plan and function most naturally and satisfactorily, namely, in his own land. A stevedore in Glasgow is in the same relation or proportion to the Scottish people as a stevedore in England to the English, or as stevedores elsewhere to peoples elsewhere. Increasing the unit does not mathematically alter the proportion. As a realist, Lenin saw this and so went into action on the basis of the organised political unit or nation of which he himself was part. He must first remould his own culture pattern and leave it to other nations to realise how valuable or otherwise the change might be.

This is the sort of fact that our more romantic internationalists do not care to face. It is so much easier to grow eloquent over the world brotherhood of the workers, their similarity of interests, and to point out that as a stevedore in London has much in common with a stevedore in Glasgow, therefore all talk of the nation as a basis for economics or art is 'nonsense'. Whatever else Lenin did, he gave the knock-out to all that. And it is only too easy to imagine a Russian today saying, 'Russian Communism, national though it be in origin, knows no frontiers and should be a common currency. ...' In such a light we can see the enormous importance of the Russian experiment. Should it work through to a permanent solution of the present appalling economic conditions in capitalist states, then humanity's indebtedness to it will be very great—and for generations literature and art may well be concerned with its spiritual interpretation and praise. Indeed, in Russia, literature and art have already been powerfully affected by the social change, though unfortunately there is no space to consider the results here, nor to look into the rebirths of arts and tongues in the various Republics. One word more in this connection. Mr Kerr says that politics and art 'are both products of contemporary life and thought', both 'no more than expressions' of the age. In an immediate sense, yes. But actually this age is the result of all the ages that have gone before. The new virile art of the working classes that Mr Kerr foresees will not be divorced from past expressions of art, but, on the contrary, will be added to them, affecting them all by its presence, as it (and they) will be affected in turn by the art of a later age.

In Ireland, the significant feature for our purpose is not economic but literary. Joyce and Yeats are not accidental portents any more than the rise of the Abbey Theatre, which responsible dramatists call the mother of Repertory in Europe. The plays of Sean O'Casey that took the theatre by storm were plays by a Dublin working man dealing realistically with the effect of a nationalist uprising on the common people. Out of conflict in the national spirit, he created his vivid drama.

There are those, of course, who put down Scotland's failure in the arts not to the loss of any possibility of conflict in the national spirit (Scotland having surrendered her nationhood and therefore all responsibility), but to the introduction of Calvinism. Could anything be more fantastic? For it only requires a moment's thought to realise that an even worse failure occurred in Ireland, which has remained Roman Catholic throughout. In metaphysics, experimental science, painting, and even in architecture, Scotland struggled along to give some sort of account of herself. By comparison, Romanist Ireland remained deep in superstition and despair. The magnificent outburst of literature in recent years in Ireland synchronised precisely with the national uprising of the people; and it is a fair assumption that had the national spirit not raised its head, the literature would not have appeared. Religion in either case was not one of the profound factors in the matter. Excess of Calvinism was a symptom, not a cause. If the loss of Catholicism was Scotland's undoing, then the history of the Scandinavian countries with their brilliant progress in literature, sculpture, and architecture must remain one of the world's great mysteries!

So far as social evolution has gone, then, it would seem that a man creates most potently within his own national environment. Outside it he is not so sure of himself, not so fertile, not so profound. That appears to be the accepted anthropological fact. Lenin recognised it. So did the Irish writers. If a man feels that he has no longer a nation of his own, then he will hang on to some other nation, as the Scottish Labour Party, for example, hangs on to the English Labour Party. Unless the English Party may be cajoled into doing something about Mr Kerr's working-class ideal, the Scots of themselves can do nothing. The relationship is essentially parasitic, working at second-hand, and provides the mechanism of escape for those who have not the courage to assume direct responsibility. For, whether we like it or not, the nation is still the basis of all large-scale creative human endeavour, and in that sense, it seems to me, it would be difficult for a Scot to show up impressively before either an Irish dramatist or a Russian of the classless state.

19

Nationalism in Writing

I—Tradition and Magic in the Work of Lewis Grassic Gibbon

Scots Magazine, 1938

> This article, on an aspect of the work of Lewis Grassic Gibbon (J Leslie Mitchell), was written by special request, shortly after that writer's death, for a projected book of similar appreciations by other writers. Gunn heard no more of the project and allowed *The Scots Magazine* to print it as the first of three articles on the general subject of Nationalism in Writing.

The two qualities in Leslie Mitchell's writing that move me to delight are his profound sense of Tradition and his eye for, and power to juggle with, Magic. These qualities I find at their most potent in *Sunset Song*; less so in the succeeding two parts of the *Quair*; and scarcely discernible in such of his purely English fiction as I have read.

Why this should be so in the case of the normal or orthodox use of English raises perhaps one of the most interesting speculations in literary practice known to our age. I am aware how unfair and misleading it can be to try to get at an author's own convictions or disabilities by way of what he has placed in the thought of one of his imagined characters, and accordingly I quote the following description of the division in the mind of the girl Chris Guthrie rather as a condition applicable to every mind that is trying to be creative in the fundamental world of the senses.

> Two Chrisses there were that fought for her heart and tormented her. You hated the land and the coarse speak of the folk and learning was brave and fine one day; and the next you'd waken with the peewits crying across the hills, deep and deep, crying in the heart of you and the smell of the earth in your face, almost you'd cry for that, the beauty of it and the sweetness of the Scottish land and skies. You saw their faces in firelight. … You wanted the words they'd known and used, forgotten in the far-off youngness of their lives, Scots words to tell to your heart how they wrung it and held it, the toil of their days and unendingly their fight. And the

next minute that passed from you, you were English, back to the English
words so sharp and clean and true—for a while, for a while, till they slid
so smooth from your throat you knew they could never say anything that
was worth the saying at all.

Thus one comes to appreciate not only the problem which Mitchell the realist
posed to himself, but his brave effort to solve it. For manifestly the difficulty that
here confronted him in all its terrible simplicity was to evoke the living girl in that
absolute way that would make her known not only to us but to herself. The 'sharp
and clean and true' refers not to evocation of such living reality but to description
in exact terms of an outer apprehended reality whether in economic or social
conditions or in the world of all the sciences.

It is a basic distinction, and one that may reasonably be taken to indicate
Mitchell's own preoccupation with life; on the one hand, the concern of the
creative artist; on the other, the concern of the man for the iniquitous conditions
of the poor, strengthened by knowledge gained from his studies in archaeology
and anthropology. Accordingly it might broadly be suggested that when Mitchell
is using orthodox English, he is manipulating intellectual rather than blood values,
and consequently in the realm of the emotions such English does not move us
with a sense of the unconditional magic of life or of that life's being rooted in the
breeding soil of tradition.

Before going on to consider more particularly the rather rash terms, Tradition
and Magic, perhaps I should look for a moment at the nature of the effort he
made to solve his problem, because it involved the use of the English language
in a new pattern. To a writer, and particularly to a Scots writer, the problem
is not only fascinating but still for the most part awaiting individual solution.
Any effort at logical analysis would, of course, require much more space than
this little essay will occupy, but if I may be allowed to cut the reasoning and
come to my conclusion, I should say that what Mitchell achieved was not a new
language but an old rhythm. Apart from a handful of Scots words, the medium
used in the Scots novels is English, but the effect produced by the rhythm is
utterly un-English. Indeed it is so profoundly of the soil of which Mitchell writes
that in an odd moment of reverie the illusion is created of the soil itself speaking.
The girl Chris realises she must have this rhythm of words or she will not know
herself; Mitchell realises it; and the earth is fecund with it as with the peewit's cry.
Mitchell makes the bold stroke of using it, and *Sunset Song* will justify him till the
peewit becomes *vanellus vulgaris* in that language of Cosmopolis towards which he
saw the whole world move.

Yet what a troubling division was in him just there! For he never imaginatively
realised this Cosmopolis; he merely accepted it, like Tennyson or Mr H G Wells,
as something in the nature of 'Progress' that is inevitable; and it was inevitable for
Mitchell, I feel, not because of any ultimate need for it *in itself*, but because it was for

humanity's final good *on the material or economic plane.* When we attain Cosmopolis, economic slavery and physical want will have vanished (though precisely why—as apart from piously—is never explained by any Cosmopolitan). It was not his anthropological studies, his scientific visualisations, if I may use such a phrase, that moved him here so much as his genuine, profoundly sensitive concern for the downtrodden; not that this concern expressed itself in the natural positive terms of love or kindness or Christian charity, but, characteristically (of himself and of his age), in a hatred of the oppressors—individual and system—that drew from him so often language of scathing directness or of obliterating irony. His sympathy is with 'the lowly, the oppressed, the Cheated of the Sunlight, the bitter relics of the savagery of the Industrial Revolution', and he 'would welcome the end of Braid Scots and Gaelic, our culture, our history, our nationhood under the heels of a Chinese army of occupation if it would cleanse the Glasgow slums, give a surety of food and play—the elementary right of every human being—to those people of the abyss'.

This conjunction of social reformer and literary artist is generally held by the critics to be disastrous to inspired imaginative creation. And on occasion it certainly betrays Mitchell, as, for example, when he brings Ewan back from an ordinary training camp in Scotland to behave to his wife in so perverted and brutal a fashion that the reader can make less of it than Chris herself; a Ewan, too, reared amid all the healthy realities of the farmlands of the Mearns and already acquainted with most human experience between seduction and self-preservation. But I feel that Mitchell's concern for the poor and his hatred of any brutalising machine of the economic oppressors are factors of such importance in his make-up as a writer that any literary lapses to which they may lead him—often through restraint arising from excess of sensibility or through the taking of the social evil for granted—are relatively insignificant. Writers of the first class can no more escape the spirit of their age than they can stand detached from its struggles. With his sympathies already committed, for a writer to think he can justly hold the balance between the revolutionary and the reactionary may no doubt flatter him into the belief that he is acting like a god, but into his judgements or descriptions falsity will inevitably be woven.

In this respect Mitchell was never static, weighing 'literary values' as if they were eternally divorced from life and change (critics who do something like this fulfil a very necessary if secondary function), but dynamic and deeply committed to human life as it was lived around him, and facing fearlessly and courageously the ominous darkness of the future. In that sense, he was a portent on the Scottish scene and to me at least a portent of incalculable potentiality.

Now, all that being wrapped up in his idea of Cosmopolis, it naturally leads him to assert that he would destroy civilisation itself if it meant food and fun for the Glasgow slum dwellers. But to whatever exaggerations or sentimentalities it may have prompted him, the *cri-de-coeur* had justice at its core, and, for that matter, if we could see the whole actuating motive, probably the dream of that Golden Age which he believed the hag-ridden rites of civilisation strangled so long ago.

From that economic-ethical standpoint it is impossible to divorce the creative writer. Nor is there any need to, for the dichotomy is apparent only, even if Mitchell does not always appear to have realised as much himself. For to us the fact is that when he came to do his first creative work he deliberately chose not a language of Cosmopolis, not even orthodox English (which is near enough to cosmopolitan size for all practical purposes), but a particular use and pattern of English applicable to a small part of the small country of Scotland, a regional rhythm—and dying at that!

Not only so, but he (in *Scottish Scene*) has a characteristically fierce onslaught on all living Scottish authors writing in English, for him they are not Scottish authors at all, but, at the best, 'brilliantly unorthodox Englishmen writing on Scotshire'. Quite apart from the 'heights of Scots literature' they do not attain even its 'pedestrian levels'.

From *economic* Cosmopolis to *creative* Nationalism, the turnabout is absolutely complete. And by his own work, it is absolutely justified. From the last ever-widening ring, he has come back in a rush to the heart of the disturbance. His rationalising of this may be faulty. In *Sunset Song*, for example, he justly recognises himself as a Scots writer attempting Scots work. But his use of English is similar in kind and creative intention to that of a considerable number of modern Irish writers, whose reputations are worldwide; to what is being produced in America; and possibly to what is being attempted in Scotland, if the mannerism was not always pronounced enough to take his fancy. But if his reasoning is inadequate here, the urge that moved him to it is sound. In a similar way his professed readiness to accept the Chinese army of occupation is sound, though at the same time palpably fantastic, simply because the Scots people, reforming and running their own social system, could cleanse the Glasgow slums without help either from the Chinese or from Cosmopolis. Why a Scot may not consume the surplus he produces until he has got the permission of an Asiatic or Cosmopolist is a mystery that is not going to remain for ever dark. I would have had more faith in Mitchell's Cosmopolis if Mitchell had shown more faith in his own Scotland, and that for the obvious reason that the chance of reforming the world becomes possible only in so far as we show a disposition to reform ourselves. If a Scot is going to help the world towards Socialism, then the place for him is Glasgow or Dundee; if towards Cosmopolism, then still Glasgow or Dundee; if towards some still finer conception, yet again his native heath. History shows that the manner in which the peoples of the world have created new systems, from the Pharaohs to Lenin, is not likely to be upset by a sudden crystallisation of that Wellsian vagueness towards some universal good which has been, very properly, the theme of dreamers in all ages.

The intention here, however, is not to argue such discrepancies in belief or logic, but rather to indicate that Mitchell's hatred of human evil in our social relations and love of human good were fundamental and inalienable, and occasionally had such an intensity as gave his spirit a singular radiance.

It is because, then, of this real knowledge of, and revolutionary attitude towards, world affairs, that Mitchell's return to the Mearns in the narrowest, most absolute way, to perform his greatest creative act, is so striking and so important. And when he came back to write out of the tradition that was native to him, he inevitably became more truly traditional than the most ardent provincial charged with local pride. The sense of our Tradition is richer in Mitchell than in almost any modern Scot I know. For he is not primarily concerned with any particular phase of it, with whether we have sprung from Ossian or Dunbar; he is not the conscious craftsman continuing and enriching some particular past greatness; he is something newer and older than all that; he is the last man bred out of the Mearns earth, and at the same time and just as realistically he is the vanished Pict; in some curious but potent way, he is himself and his own reincarnation.

Thay may sound vague, but, taken in conjunction with what we have already said of his social ideas, it illuminates, I hope, his attitude to the whole range of Scottish history. For, above all, Mitchell feels himself as the man who roamed and tilled out Scottish land, its 'common man', who endured the conqueror, the tyranny that bred war and famine and plague, from century to century, epoch to epoch, but through it all turned to earth and sea, and from what was everlasting bred what is everlasting in us.

Accordingly it becomes easy to apprehend his meaning when he sees the Celts as 'a conquering military caste not a people in migration … They survive to the present day as a thin strand in the Scottish population … They were and remain one of the greatest curses of the Scottish scene … It is one of the strangest jests in history that they should have given their name to so much that is fine and noble.' And: 'If the Kelts were the first great curse of Scotland, the Norse were assuredly the second … And yet those dull, dyspeptic, whey-faced clowns have figured in all orthodox histories as the bringers of something new and vital to Scottish culture. …'

No doubt his method of expression is deliberately meant to provoke complacent Scots, and, in any case, there are other historic readings of Celt and Norseman. M Hubert, for example, in two exhaustive books on the rise and decline of the Celts, shows them as being driven continually to the West, because 'they were not conquerors, they were civilisers'. But again, as in the dream of Cosmopolis, the debatable points are unimportant over against the validity of what Mitchell is striving to establish. And here is its picture: 'The peasant at his immemorial toil would lift his eyes to see a new master installed at the broch, at the keep, at, later, the castle: and would shrug the matter aside as one of indifference, turning, with the rain in his face, to the essentials of existence, his fields, his cattle, his woman in the dark little eirde, earth-house.' And when Christianity came he 'merely exchanged the bass chanting of the Druid in the pre-Druid circles for the whining hymnings of priests in wood-built churches: and turned to his land again'.

There is something deeper in all this than sympathy keyed to violence for the common man who has eternally to endure. For Mitchell believed, in common with a modern school devoted to scientific research in anthropology, that before civilisation came to ride us, there did exist on earth what the poets have called a Golden Age. That belief was at the back of his mind giving it poise and philosophy, impetus and wrath. And whether (as with his Cosmopolis and racial judgements) it is right or wrong again does not greatly matter to our purpose, for man has in him to this day a positive intuition of that far-back primordial goodness. Mitchell knew it not only scientifically but in the marrow of the bone.

Tradition is, then, for him at once a living embodiment of racial history and of his own history; and its settings (as in Chris's innermost thought) is 'the sweetness of the Scottish land and skies'. True to his instinct, he sets down the tale of it in the speech, the living rhythm, of the common man who in that land still endures.

Yet, however true his knowledge and intuition of Tradition, that tale would be unexceptional as literature if not touched, as we say, by creative fire. And so we arrive at last at what I may too spontaneously have called Magic. But this is where I want to please myself and to admit my own delight!

It is easy to say that Mitchell is a poet; and only a trifle less easy to argue that the degree of poetic inspiration is the measure of the novelist. We have the orthodox English conceptions of character-creation and descriptive narrative, and these are used by Mitchell as a matter of course and superbly well; but I maintain that the delight he communicates is something beyond this, beyond narration of seedtime and harvest in earth and brute; beyond a last human concern for the girl Chris Guthrie even; it is the transfusing spirit or essence of these and all that goes to give them substance and texture in a living and eternal pattern, and it is evoked by what I can only think of at the moment as incantation. And it is because (even to the precise degree in which) this evocative quality is lacking in *Cloud Howe* and *Grey Granite* that they fall short of *Sunset Song*. Any critical concern for exaggeration of fact or overstatement of brutality or limitation of style or other arguable detail of his work is here of quite secondary importance, is indeed almost beside the point. By virtue of this particular vision Mitchell gave reality to his earth and all that moved thereon against the eternal background. And if this savours of the easy phrase, *sub specie aeternatatis,* let me again repeat that the eternity was quite specifically the Tradition which I have so inadequately tried to suggest. For example, he is never overcome by fear or curiosity or mental blankness in the middle of a Stone Circle. He sees himself moving there in the twilights beyond recorded history, and occasionally seems to convey the scene by his very presence, without a word. He calls a place the 'den of Kinraddie', and the syllables are not only troubling in an evocative, prehistoric, wild-beast fashion, but cunningly draw into them, like prey, the starkest cries from the ballads. The Grampians are seen through a dip in the ground or a pass in the trees, and the face of the girl bears the wonder and strange delight and half-fear of all the faces that have so gazed since time began.

Finally, in this apprehension of what our Tradition is and what its evocation may mean in the way of delight, there is 'something still more deeply interfused'. I can only refer vaguely here to a richness, a fecundity, out of which life itself is born and will go on being born. For meaning, we should have to get contrasts—with, for instance, what it is that keeps some of our moderns burrowing among the roots. Whatever of darkness or sourness is in the Mearns soil, however the roots twist or knot, the white shoot of life pierces upward to the sun. There need be no lack of complexity, of thought coiling on itself like a druidic serpent, but the inherent principle is always that of life, never of the perversity that leads, by convolutions fascinating because personal, to the sterility that is ultimate death. So obvious a statement of opposites does not naturally permit mention of D H Lawrence, yet a profound study might well be made of what Lawrence hunted for in the deeps and contrasted with what Mitchell at least indicated might be born out of our Scottish soil in all its long pedigree from the sun circles of the pre-Druids: indeed, from long before that, when the life principle, working through perfect health, had for a spell its Golden Age.

Some time ago a distinguished Scottish writer, broadcasting on the efforts of his brethren, suggested that our Scottish countryside had nothing more to give the indigenous novelist. As if it were a place that had been skinned, leaving the void beneath. How effectively Mitchell proceeded to show that so far hardly even the skin had been affected! How supremely tragic that the demonstration should then have ceased!

20

Nationalism in Writing

II—The Theatre Society of Scotland

Scots Magazine, 1938

I have just received a circular from the secretary of a new association which is in process of being formed with a view to establishing 'an endowed professional theatre in Scotland'. I have been interested from time to time in so many new 'movements' within our country, and have got so used to seeing them run their short race and fade out, that my first approach to still another effort is inclined to be tinged with scepticism.

I think I am expressing there a general attitude, an attitude which is almost instinctive and therefore rarely analysed. For, in the first place, why should Scotland be suffering this lust for new movements, and, in the second, why should we approach them with a touch of scepticism or despair?

To answer these two questions with anything approaching fullness or adequacy would require at least a whole issue of this magazine, because obviously it would entail a careful and realist investigation into what the word Scotland sums up in itself; and only when we arrived at that should we be in a position to appreciate what elements of the whole were so being denied or inhibited that every now and then there had to be efforts at easing or evacuating the congestion by 'movements'. This may have the air of being a too physiological parallel for what may appear to be a psychological affair. But in fact it is not so, for associations or parties, aiming at the freedom of the body politic, have been more strongly at work, have received greater publicity and have been better organised than any associations working for a cultural expression. I do not say that they have been more important, for body and mind make a single working unit and neither can function without the other.

But manifestly I cannot go into all that here. Even if space permitted, we should very soon hardly be able to see the green for bonnets! For the last thing we are prepared to do in a matter of this kind is to regard it scientifically. When a doctor sees a man suffering from nerves or on the verge of a break-down, he does not consider it unnecessary to ask him a few questions about his bodily health.

Yet that same doctor, if he is a literary gentleman, aware of Scotland's mental or artistic deficiencies, will at once pooh-pooh the very idea that the causal factors may lie in the governance or functioning of poor old Scotland's body. He affects to be superior to those who do consider the body, deems them cranks or quacks, and wise-cracks at their expense. All of which is very easy and entertaining, but of no earthly use as diagnosis. For he dare not face up to a scientific diagnosis. None of us really cares to be told the truth if it is going to be in the least uncomfortable. Better let us slide on as we are doing, and if we can be eased now and then by a new 'movement', particularly if it is cultural, why we are doing fine!

That, as far as I can make out, is the general Scottish attitude to-day. That it is an uneasy attitude, covering a feeling that something internal and deep-seated is far wrong, is, as I suggest, manifest from these sporadic ebullitions of energy that every now and then conceive a new weekly, monthly or quarterly journal, a new amateur, national or repertory theatre, a new political organisation or link-up of existing organisations, a new analysis, a new poetry, a new Highland League, a new rebellion, a new desperation of some sort. These symptoms are known and declared. They are not fanciful.

And the latest is this effort to form a 'Theatre Society of Scotland'. Those who first conceived the project obviously made up their minds that it was to be no hole-and-corner affair of parochial enthusiasm. Apparently the conception of Scotland is widening. Even in 'movements', there is no avoiding the general law of learning from our mistakes and defeats. After all, presumably it is a big affair or nothing; it is of national size, with inter-national implications, or it isn't worth bothering about. So amongst patron advisers, we find names like Ashley Dukes of London, Hilton Edwards of the Gate Theatre, Dublin, Tyrone Guthrie now of the Old Vic; in organisation, names of University principals, and of city fathers like Will Y Darling and P J Dollan: in playwriting, Bridie and Robins Millar; in literature, Eric Linklater, Hugh MacDiarmid, Edwin Muir, to select a contrasted trio; and so on for painting, sculpture, and the learned professions. Of the long list of printed names, only a small minority is Scottish Nationalist in politics. It is as if it had been decided to approach the national problem from the inter-national point of view.

Now, let me make it quite quite clear that the promoters do not explicitly recognise a 'national problem' at all. In their prospectus there is no suggestion that Scotland needs a theatre through which she may express her essential self. They merely want to 'bring together all who believe in the social and artistic value of the theatre, in order that a united effort may be made to establish an endowed professional theatre in Scotland.' This theatre 'would form a permanent centre for the pleasure of audiences and the advancement of the art of the theatre'. Amongst its services to the community, it would 'explore the theatrical possibilities of Scottish intonation and movement, as shown in national speech and dance' and 'interest Scottish artists and art students in the work of scene and costume design'. 'Plays of all nations, types and tendencies' would be performed, as well as ballet, opera, and even the right sort of revue.

In short, what is envisaged here is a professional theatre for Scotland, through which the whole art of the stage would be made manifest; a national theatre such as countries of less population than Scotland, and with very much less material resources and educational endowment, possess normally in Europe. Even down in the Balkans, where a city may not have half the population of Edinburgh and a tiny fraction of its wealth, one naturally looks for its Opera House or its National Theatre. From the Balkans to Norway, where every budding dramatist thinks in terms of Ibsen. And from Norway to Dublin, where the endowed Abbey Theatre has produced drama that has had no small effect in recent years in revivifying the English stage and in setting a certain fashion to Europe.

Surely it should be possible to endow one such theatre in Scotland. Think of Glasgow with its enormous population and industrial wealth—the boasted second city of the earth's greatest empire—and then think of it or its citizens unwilling to endow one small theatre. For the moment, do not let us quarrel over the reason for this. Let us simply realise the fact, and see in this Theatre Society a body of Scottish men and women, representative of all the arts and of learning, endeavouring to bring an endowed Scottish theatre into being. Anyone can join this Society by paying half a crown and so help to realise the great aim. Are we capable of doing it?

As I began by saying, my first reaction was one of scepticism. But there are factors undoubtedly favourable to the scheme. The idea of Scotland as a unit for such an experiment is emerging. The swift and vast spread of the Community Drama Festival Movement implies that we have been starved of true dramatic nourishment. And there is, in satisfaction of what I have called the general Scottish attitude, the negative factor that the scheme is not 'nationalist'. For all those who assert that political nationalism is nonsense, and that what we want is a purely cultural revival, then here surely is their perfect opportunity to prove their case in at least one direction, that of the drama. Will they do it? Those of us who incline to scepticism, because of an analysis of the Scottish situation such as I have earlier indicated, shall await the results with interest: and meantime, let it be said, shall assist in every way possible.

For we in Scotland are labouring under difficulties. In Dublin, Irish national life was so strong that it created a drama out of itself. It had not to appeal to patrons by promising foreign plays and ballet and opera. It did not say: Endow us so that we may give you artistic satisfactions. It said: We will show you your own life translated into drama, and make you sit up, and look at it, and realise it as you have never done before. Here is Ireland, here is Cathleen ni Hoolihan, here are your conflicts and your slums, the plough and the stars, and there goes the all-wise Juno, and there her drunken Paycock asking: 'What is the moon; what is the stars?' I have seen most of the great Abbey plays in the Abbey, and remember vividly still the shock I got when, at my first visit many years ago, I heard the Irish voices in the 'Shadow of a Gunman' coming over the footlights into the darkened auditorium. I had forgotten, if I had ever known, that contemporary drama could act on one like this.

But we cannot expect anything like that in Scotland, because there has been neither a sense of national conflict nor of national travail; there has not been that high movement of the country's spirit out of which great drama is made. That is not a vague emotional statement; it is simple fact, and can be checked, as I say, by reference to the experience of Ireland and, even still more recently, by the experience of Russia and the remarkable drama that is appearing in that country, a drama that makes most of our British pieces look like sophisticated trifling about sweet or nasty nothings.

How, then, can an endowed theatre in Scotland be of any real use to us, apart of course from providing those so-called artistic satisfactions? Where dramatic conflict is lacking how can real drama emerge? What do we want a national theatre for if we have nothing in ourselves, nothing national, to express there?

In a sentence, is this to be another petit-bourgeois effort at keeping abreast of other peoples' conceptions of the drama of life? Looking ahead, I think not. Because of our position, as I have attempted to hint at it, we need a theatre first, to which Scottish writers may bring their conceptions of life, born out of a heredity and environment peculiarly their own. These conceptions may be defeatist, disruptive, rebellious, constructive, but at least they would refer to elements of conflict in our country that are profoundly real, from the tragic and heroic sea-fisheries of the north to the desperate industrialism of the south, from the Highland glen to the Lowland farm, with all the vital inter-play of character and thought and aspiration such scenes inevitably imply, for portrayal through the essential Scottish conception of fantasy, comedy, and tragedy. At present a Scottish writer has no theatre to which he can take any such drama. Just as his country suffers from having no focal point, no vitalising heart, so the native playwright suffers, in this single element of the drama, from having no central stage, no national theatre, to which he may bring the fruits of his talent and have them read and judged as drama, not as hopeful commercial efforts at understudying the London stage. Even in the immense growth of the Community Drama Festival Movement, he has proved to himself already that only a certain type of play is preferred for competitive purposes. To a large degree it has become a game of acquiring marks, and the more cunning amateurs have become expert at the game.

What the Scottish playwright, who feels he may have something to say or to evoke, needs is a theatre, run by professional players, to whom he can entrust the expression of adult thought and irony and imagination. Without such a theatre he is crippled in expression or simply does not write plays at all and turns to some other medium, like the novel. Such a theatre needs to be endowed, if we are going to get the best.

Again let it be said that this Theatre is not being founded with a view to encouraging the Scottish playwright. It will encourage him for all that, and the seeing of first-class foreign work will be no disadvantage to a developing technique. If he comes away with plays, as the Irish and Russians have done, there will be much more fun going around than is usually found in a milieu for providing social and artistic values. But that smile must remain directed towards the lap of the gods.

Meanwhile there are doubting but still hopeful Scots who will watch with considerable interest what is going to happen to the Theatre Society of Scotland.

21

Nationalism in Writing
III – Is Scottish Individualism to be Deplored?

Scots Magazine, 1939

How often is it stated in these days that what is wrong with the Scot is his individualism! Because of this characteristic, this inbred desire to gang his ain gait, he is the notorious creator of schism. The history of his Church appears to show it conclusively, for surely if there is any realm in which a people with a long tradition should tend to be at one it is in the religious, where no personal privilege should intrude and all vanities be forgotten; yet the divisions and sub-divisions in the history of Scottish worship have been more numerous and bitter than those in the history of almost any other country. Again, in the temporal sphere, there is much the same record of sporadic communal endeavour destroyed by internal bickerings or lack of faith, whether it be a scheme of co-operation in the Western Highlands that runs its short course and dies, or the effort to-day at a political and economic reintegration of the whole nation which can hardly be said to have roused popular enthusiasm. Indeed, it has become a common saying that the Scot can govern anyone but himself. Even when he did combine, as the crofters combined towards the end of last century to fight for a common aim and had their victory recorded on the statute book, what was won was the right of each individual crofter to security of tenure. That end ensured, those concerned immediately reverted to an individualism which can hardly be considered to have saved the Highlands economically or spiritually.

So much has all this been the case, that our best Scottish writers to-day not only deplore it, but turn away from any particular consideration of the Scottish scene towards more hopeful movements of the human spirit in other countries.

The whole theme is one of great interest and deep importance. In fact, it may be said that the conception of individualism, of individual freedom, is occupying the mind of man to-day more sharply than at any other period.

Freedom is a word that is used frequently, yet seldom defined. Its meaning is taken for granted. Now the danger in taking anything for granted is not altogether that it may produce a confusion in thought. We may all have approximate agreement in the meaning. The danger lies in assuming as inevitably correct those basic conditions—the premises—out of which the meaning or accepted conception is born.

In the ancient agrarian system there was the relationship of the master and the slave. To us, more familiarly, there were the feudal lord and the serf. Here was a human relationship in a form of society so circumscribed that it had a clear pattern, with laws of conduct and social obligations very simply defined. The serf found his freedom in complete dependence on his master, much as soldiers in a modern army are said to find freedom in dependence on their officers (that is, in getting rid of all responsibility for personal decisions), or as members of a Church may find freedom by resigning the purpose of their lives into its absolving and saving hands.

Now the ancient agrarian system might have continued indefinitely, for it was essentially static, were it not for that discontent in man which is sometimes called divine. Man began to adventure, to trade, to gather wealth that he held on to as his own. In thus adventuring and trading he found the horizons of the world opening out before him, and the inner horizons of his thought widening beyond his dreams. New speculations, new beauty, and, in particular, a new and thrilling conception of personal freedom. It was as if he had been born again; and, in fact, this new attitude to life came to be called the Renaissance. Enter the trader, the merchant, the financier—the new bourgeois class.

The old personal relationship in the agrarian state was now seen to be intolerable in its human compulsion. No man should have absolute power over another man, as the master had over the slave, or the lord over his serf. The consequent servility denied the God-implanted spirit in man and lowered him to the level of the beast of burden. Man had been born free, but everywhere (as Rousseau memorably summed it up) he was in chains. The chains must be broken and man emerge as master of his fate and captain of his soul. Man's high destiny was to be independent of any man's compulsion, and he was, in fact, completely free only when he could withdraw from society altogether and pursue his thought or his wild flowers or his loves in some happy bower far from the multitude's ignoble strife.

This bourgeois society which followed on the gradual break-up of the agrarian or feudal system, and which is still with us, has been for man the most brilliant period in his history. It brought tremendous gains in speculative thought, wealth, diversity of art and applied art, diffusion of knowledge, travel and adventure, but particularly in science and mechanics, and to such a degree that it fully discovered and in no small measure changed the surface of the earth. The enterprise and energy expended were stupendous and in result often magnificent and sometimes marvellous. It is doubtful indeed whether the tyranny that underlay the old feudal system could have been broken by any less powerful force. It certainly was broken, and man emerged, a free individual with control over his destiny.

Of course, there was one respect in which he was not free, namely in his economic relations, but then he never can be free there so long as his animal body needs food, shelter and clothing. That had all along been realised. But bourgeois society had provided in some measure for that difficulty, too, by offering the opportunity to a small percentage of its members to amass wealth or property, so that without toiling or spinning themselves they could yet be housed and fed. The right to achieve this happy state was denied to none. The basis of the whole system was equal opportunity and equal right under the law. No man could compel any other man's labour. Every man was free to offer his labour or to withhold it, to stay at home or to adventure abroad. The old relationship that had existed between the lord and serf was dissolved and its place taken by a cash relationship.

This change from the personal to the impersonal was bound to be fraught with striking consequences, because the one fact about economic or social relations is that they are social; that is, human. If they are dehumanised, then the emotional forces of man are interfered with and, lacking normal expression, will in course of time, and after many rumblings, find abnormal expression; particularly if, behind them, is the growing compulsion of economic necessity.

And this in truth began to happen. Man had won free from the direct tyranny of man by accepting the indirect tyranny of cash. But because the tyranny of cash appeared indirect, it was no less compulsive than the tyranny of the slave owner, for without cash in this fine new world, man dies. In truth, the machine that employed him, when it was glutted, threw him aside—unlike the old master who continued to look after his slave because, at the lowest, he was of value to him, as was his horse.

A strange new world indeed, where man in theory was completely free and where yet in practice he found himself tied by invisible chains to a machine. If he threw off the chains, he starved. He was free to starve. But no man wants to starve, nor does he want his wife and children to starve. And then a new horror invaded this hitherto expanding and adventuring society: the difficulty of finding a machine to which to chain himself. Slumps, unemployment, war.

II

So this new society began to be examined with some care. It professed the complete freedom of the individual, a freedom that was as much his birth-right as it was that of any noble animal of the forest. Free trade. Free thought. There seemed no end to this freedom—until one man came up against another man's property and found that (unlike the noble animal of the forest in parallel circumstances) he was not free to attempt to acquire it by stealth or force, however much he required it and however little the owner did. A man—every man—had not only the right to hold to what was his own, but was supported in that right by the laws of bourgeois society. The machine might appear a very impersonal thing, but it was private property. And the man who owned it had as much power over the man who worked it for him as ever lord had over his serf—but not a direct, personal power, for the human relationships had been lost in the cash nexus. This was a very interesting discovery and gave rise to all sorts of political doctrines and economic analyses. To 'blame' the man who owned the machine was absurd. It was implicit in the system that men should own the machines and that men should work them.

Once again then it seemed that, though man had been born free, he was still everywhere in chains. Bourgeois society had, in fact, failed to give man the individual freedom that it conceived of as his birthright. What had gone wrong? Or was bourgeois society doomed by its very nature to be unable to give it to him?

The answer to this, from the new school of thought that now divides the world, was the striking one that bourgeois society could not give it to him because its very conception of freedom was itself a myth. Man was not 'born free' in the Rousseau sense. Man was not a lonely, splendid being who 'found his soul' only when he withdrew from society and all its dealings. Man, as we know him, could fulfil himself and find his highest measure of freedom only in and through society; man was a social animal, not a detached and noble individual independent of all restraint.

This was indeed revolutionary doctrine, hitting not only at our bourgeois conceptions of society, but at some of its finest literature, at most of its speculative thought, and at not a little of its scientific research. Its argument against being 'born free' for example, was as simple as this: Take the child when he is 'born free' and send him out to the wilds to be suckled by goat or ewe, and then visit him after twenty years to see what sort of man he has grown into. Even the most optimistic would hardly expect him to have speech, music, art, science, poetry, in any developed form! In short, that which distinguishes us from the animal, that which gives us the very power to contemplate freedom as a possible possession, is received from society.

This was the new doctrine, derived from Karl Marx. It was not only an economic creed: it was a whole way of living, a philosophy of life, and many of its devotees profess their faith with a religious zeal. Bourgeois society, with its private ownership of the sources of production, had not only failed to satisfy the economic needs of society, with consequent slumps, unemployment and war, but in the process had driven man into a tyrannical impersonal relationship to a machine instead of into a warm, human relationship happily held together by common economic necessity. Absolute freedom was a myth. Even the owner of the machine was not free. His economic privileges were the result of a constant watchfulness, and often indeed of slavish, fear-driven hard work.

The important psychological element in this new doctrine was, of course, the tender social relations that would exist between men who in common owned the means of economic production. To satisfy a common need there would be a common endeavour, divorced from any possibility of private tyranny. In this endeavour man would find his freedom, the greatest measure of freedom he can ever hope to find; for as an animal he must always be under the compulsion of economic necessity and as an individual he can get his culture only from society. The economic relations that are the basis of society thus became of supreme importance. An individualism which tended to disrupt economic relations, which challenged this new social doctrine, had to be squashed for the common good. And the proof of the doctrine was always to be discovered by working it out in actual practice. That was part of what was called its dialectic: one thinks and then one acts, and the validity of the thought is proved or otherwise in the action.

If in bourgeois society the important element was the individual, in this new conception of society the important thing was society itself, based always and forever on economic relations.

III

Now this new doctrine came to be tested in actual practice in Russia and with results that have in many ways been remarkable. But it is not the intention here to enumerate economic achievements, or to express a personal attitude to the Russian experiment. Our immediate point of interest lies in this matter of individual freedom, and it has to be recorded that, more and more, responsible critics are beginning to wonder whether in this particular respect the doctrine is really proving itself in practice. I refer particularly, perhaps necessarily, to critics who themselves were favourable to the experiment and anxious for its fulfilment, such a critic as Mr Herbert Read, who, in his recent book, *Poetry and Anarchism*, has come to the conclusion that all is not well in Russia so far as this personal freedom is concerned. He makes allowances for the necessary suppressions of the 'transition period', but regretfully finds that after twenty-one years the suppressive and repressive influences are still at work, and twenty-one years is a long time. For it was a cardinal part of the original doctrine that after the transition period, after a classless society had been achieved, then the conjunction of forces which had achieved it would naturally tend to disappear; or, as it was graphically put by Engels, the State would gradually 'wither away'. But Mr Read finds that the State in this case, instead of showing any signs of withering away, is, on the contrary, growing stronger, with everywhere its bureaucratic forces becoming more solidly entrenched. Freedom of individual expression and action remains restricted, and the tragic fate of some of the Revolution's best poets and writers leaves him deeply troubled. For, unless the State withers away, Communism to Mr Read is merely another tyranny, the tyranny of the bureaucrat over the worker, and he finds it difficult to believe that the tyranny is likely to grow less, because of the psychological factor that *power corrupts*.

And no matter how perfectly in these circumstances the economic life of the country is arranged, such a critic as Mr Read would still be unimpressed, because the best example of a perfect functioning of economic relations is to be found in the beehive—a conception of efficiency that applied to human society would be utterly repulsive.

The freedom of the individual would thus seem to be an elusive quality! Yet nothing is more certain than that individual man, with his capacity for rational decision, is the highest-known achievement of the evolutionary process. First the single cell, multiplying itself by fission. Then the grouping of cells in a single organism in a relationship that may be regarded as rigidly economic. The increasing complexity of the organism, with functional specialisation of parts, until man arrives on the scene, and adds to the economic relations the new element of self-consciousness, the human mind. This new element, this 'extra dimension', of the organism, is particularly distinguished by its capacity to discuss 'free will', to contemplate itself and ask in how far as an individual it is 'free'. Even from a purely scientific standpoint it is no wonder, then, that man should be so preoccupied with this notion or problem of freedom, for it is the flowering of the whole biological process.

Thus is set up the stress between economic relations on one side and freedom on the other. As they are interdependent, or as one arises and can only arise out of the other, there should ideally be no stress, or as little stress as possible, and so man strives to found his 'perfect State' where such a happy arrangement might be consummated. But because of the complex nature of man's mind, of its many elements destructive as well as constructive, and because of the basic need for economic security (with the strife and consequent greed and hate hitherto arising therefrom), he naturally finds it difficult to achieve this happy arrangement. But he goes on striving; and the business of the artist or creative writer is to see that, whatever permutations and combinations of economic relations may arise, the flower of freedom must be preserved; and not only preserved, but cultivated. In its many forms and colouring, and in the irrational subjective fantasies to which it gives rise, he finds what he calls beauty. This is the true function of artist or poet and perhaps explains the reason for the remarkable importance he has had in human history. He is the jealous guardian of the latest manifestations of individual life in the biological process.

Accordingly it would seem that he cannot become the politician in the accepted sense. He can belong to a political party and work for it in the hope that it may so arrange economic relations as to help towards human freedom, but at the same time he must forever be critical, and when he sees his party laying so much stress on economic relations that the flower of freedom is endangered, then he must protest.

IV

If, after this somewhat lengthy over-simplification of certain historic processes, we return to our original question, whether Scottish individualism is to be deplored, we may perhaps get a slightly clearer idea of the scope of the answer. At once, then, we may agree that an excessive individualism tending to neglect and disrupt the economic relations of society is harmful ultimately to individual freedom. And this, in fact, is what has happened in Scotland. But—and now the point has to be emphasised—that does not mean that individualism (the expression of individuality) is bad in itself. On the contrary, as we have seen, it marks the highest point in biological evolution, and to attempt to 'sink it' in an earlier phase—and a purely economic relationship is the earliest phase of all—would be to retrogress. In short, it is not the Scot's individualism that is at fault, it is his failure to deal with the abiding problem of economic necessity in such a socially co-operative way that he would attain the maximum freedom to develop that very individualism which as things are, seems to be his curse.

Why has he failed to do this? Does his history show him to have lagged behind in social evolution, compared with his European neighbours? The answer is very definitely in the negative. Scotland was perhaps the first country in northern Europe to give clear expression in a political instrument to the modern conception of democracy, of the 'liberty which no good man loseth but with his life'. (The Declaration of Arbroath, 1320 A.D.) Even in that earlier form of agrarian society, characterised elsewhere by the master and the slave, or the feudal lord and the serf, Scotland had a relationship between what we may loosely call chief and clansman that was not only warm and human but remarkable for a high degree of individual independence and absence of personal compulsion or tyranny. Nor was that merely 'a tribal stage', as has been made clear by those who have studied what is called the old Gaelic Commonwealth. Accordingly the institutions that grew out of this background were at an early date democratic in form, as the constitution of her Church and her legal and educational systems clearly show. What then went wrong with the evolution of Scotland *along her own natural lines* towards a higher communal integration of economic relations and a clearer expression of individual freedom? How were the chiefs debauched and turned into bad feudal lords? (for feudalism proper had a clear philosophy of its own). Why should a Clydeside communist have to turn to Russia—to Russia that, a generation ago under the Czars, was still largely at that agrarian stage of master and slave which had been transcended by Scotland before the beginning of her recorded history (if indeed it ever obtained)? Why should the Scot have retained in so marked a degree his individualism, his uneasy individualism, and lost his capacity for economic co-operation?

Does the logical answer lie in the possibility that the Scot was inevitably doomed to lose his capacity for co-operation from the very moment that he abdicated his power to deal with his own economic relations?

But that would require a searching inquiry into comparatively recent history, and so here for the time being I must let the matter rest.

22

Scottish Renaissance

Scottish Field, 1962

When I was asked to pay this personal tribute to Hugh MacDiarmid, my mind went back to the early days of our association, and I thought it might interest readers if I said something from my own experience about what has been called the Scottish Literary Renaissance and of Hugh MacDiarmid's connection with its beginnings.

I seem to remember that the appellation itself was of French origin, and certainly MacDiarmid in these years, the twenties, was in contact with French writers like Denis Saurat, and generally was very much aware of what was going on in literary affairs, particularly of a new or revolutionary kind, on the Continent. Also, of course, he had his English contacts, as I have just verified by looking up *Contemporary Scottish Studies*, by C M Grieve, and finding that the volume had belonged to Gordon Bottomley (who bequeathed his Scottish books to me), and finding further, behind the front cover, some cuttings from Glasgow newspapers showing Grieve on the warpath and dealing out everything but mercy to those who had dared question his critical judgements on contemporary Scottish writing. Clearly, then, there was one English poet of the time whose interest in Hugh MacDiarmid even went beyond the Lallans.

These cuttings had me laughing once again when, in his reply to William Power's high challenge to formulate 'a canon of criticism', he writes that, while agreeing with the need for such a canon, 'I cannot conceive of one which, to say the least of it, is simpler to expound than the theory of Relativity, and I could not attempt to formulate one myself in less space than a complete issue of the *Daily Record*'. Even as it was his reply was spread over three columns. But the exaggerated humour, the wild gesture for its own sake, was part of the adventure of that time, and the adventure was young and full of life and noise and hope.

However what I found among the cuttings and had quite forgotten was a leaflet published by the *Scottish Educational Journal* announcing a series of articles by Mr C M Grieve 'which would discuss in all the work of no fewer than three hundred men and women of Scotland in Literature, Music, Art, Drama, Education, and other branches of cultural activity ... a real achievement in nationalistic integration'. How far the promise in that formidable announcement was fulfilled may be judged by the contents of *Contemporary Scottish Studies.* For I am not concerned now with critical assessments, but only with the desire to point out and emphasise something truly astonishing, namely, the amount of sheer hard labour, of tireless discriminating research, that the completion of this work had involved.

Then let it be remembered that in these early years he was also producing Scots poetry on the level of the old Scottish masters, not to mention editing periodicals like *The Scottish Chapbook, The Northern Review* and *The Scottish Nation.* Over all, then, is it any wonder that to many Hugh MacDiarmid *was* the Scottish Literary Renaissance?

Yet that would be to exaggerate, if not to nullify, the true situation as Grieve saw it then and tried to make it clear. Indeed his articles and editings would have been pointless, unless there had been in Scotland sufficient activity and accomplishment in cultural affairs to warrant his use of a word like Renaissance. As the *S E Journal* leaflet put it: 'The synopsis given overleaf lends substance to Mr Grieve's claim that Scotland has at no time in the past had so remarkable a body of writers and artists as at the present moment, and the youth and ascending aim of the great majority of these justifies the hope that we are on the verge of a genuine awakening.'

In how far the hope was realised may be a matter for discussion (as it so often has been), but once again I wish to stress here what one man indubitably *did* to help to justify the hope and bring about a genuine awakening. Amid the national tendency towards arguments and flytings, how rare to find the doer, and particularly on so high a level over so wide a field.

But there still remains one more aspect of this unusual tale of achievement, which to-day may need special emphasis, and this is the earnestness with which at that time he strove to discover and praise good work by his contemporaries. Some of his assessments and prophecies may well be considered over-generous, as when he said somewhere in these *Studies* that there were ten living Scottish poets who were immeasurably superior to all but the ten greatest poets our race had produced throughout the past. And he named the living ten. Acclamation could hardly have gone further.

If at times denunciation went equally far in the other direction at least let it be remembered that his critical standards were indicated and that in any age indifferent work is much greater in quantity than fine work. But, that apart, what always springs spontaneously out of his research is his pleasure when he finds what he likes, first for its own sake and then for its strengthening of the Scottish national tradition in literature over against all other national traditions, particularly the one south of the Border.

Perhaps if one could define 'what he likes' some understanding might be gained of the counter-attacks he naturally enough drew upon himself. To do this briefly would be difficult. But at least it can be indicated that in the twenties a profound revolution was taking place in literature, and that it was possible for writers living in even the remoter parts of Scotland to be aware of it. One can remember reading the Parisian magazine *Transition* in the Highlands, when James Joyce's *Work* in *Progress* was appearing in its pages, and memories of some of its more intolerant avant-garde verse and denunciatory attitudes can still spill over into mirth. But it wasn't even necessary to go abroad, for T S Eliot and Ezra Pound were publishing their poetry and criticism in London. The revolution was in fact so widespread and relentless that it did not take so very long for many to feel something like a sense of secret shame for once upon a time having wallowed in Shelley or Tennyson. I knew no one in Scotland at that time who was more aware of this and more attracted by its innovations than Christopher Grieve.

So far I have been concerned with describing events that happened in these early years of the Renaissance Movement and showing how closely our poet, critic, and controversialist was identified with them. But all along at the back of my mind has been the desire to pay him, on this special occasion, a more personal tribute out of abundant memories of our joint doings and discussions, of all-night sessions when the speech organs had to be wetted now and then with a drop of old malt. His happy references to these sessions in a recent broadcast stirred the memories up, and I confess that what astonished me most, on reflection, was an absence of any real disagreement between us that I can remember as though some kind of overriding harmony held us both. Perhaps he explained at least one aspect of this when he said that our concern was to try to bridge the gulf between the Gaelic and lowland elements and so bring on a modern Scottish literature. Though no explanations can ever evoke the warm spirit of fellowship in adventure.

23

Review of *Scott and Scotland*

Scots Magazine, 1936

Literary Criticism of the quality of Mr Muir's is rare in any country; in Scotland even its tradition seems to have, got lost. In saying as much, I am not concerned with particular attributes of penetration or insight, with individual gifts of para-dox or brilliant exposition, but with that rare power of lifting criticism on to a plane where its observations and judgements combine in a synthesis that induces in the mind a state of harmony. His writing has, in fact, no tricks at all. It is quiet and lucid, and eschews colour and personal whim to the point of seeming cold. Nor is this the clarity of intellect alone. Metaphysicians are common enough. Behind Mr Muir's assessments is not only a fine intellect but an imagination of a very pure kind, and it is with the help of this imagination (or in its light) that his intellect is able to select all important factors (an intellect that included everything would describe nothing) and to combine them with the same sort of satisfying or harmonious effect as is achieved by any truly creative work. Whether his intellect is powerful or his imagination profound does not arise here. It is enough that his literary criticism is of this creative kind, because in Scotland we had almost for-gotten that real criticism was anything but a collieshangie or a fight.

Accordingly what Mr Muir may have to say on Scott and on Scotland will not only command our respect, but—more important—move us beforehand to an agreeable expectancy. If therefore I find him at the end of his present task stumbling and uncertain, it is with a feeling of dismay. It is as if when he leaves the realm of literary criticism, where his judgements are so sure and illuminating, and faces the common light of our political day, his powers of apprehension desert him. This is so curious a phenomenon that it justifies, I hope, particular attention. For the rest I can but trust that any remarks of mine may serve the one purpose of sending readers to this searching and original study of the predicament of the Scottish writer.

At once Mr Muir sees that the line his enquiry must take is not what Scott did for Scotland but what Scotland failed to do for Scott and why. How does it come about that 'by far the greatest creative force in Scottish literature as well as one of the greatest in English' leaves a feeling of 'curious emptiness' behind all the wealth of imagination? 'Many critics have acknowledged this blemish in Scott's work,' and Mr Muir sets himself out to account for it by considering the country in which Scott lived, a country 'which was neither a nation nor a province', and had, 'instead of a centre, a blank, an Edinburgh'. Scott had no country and no continuing tradition in the way that an Englishman or a German had. To this day, if a Scots writer wishes to add something to his native literature, 'he will find in Scotland, no matter how long he may search, neither an organic community to round off his conceptions, nor a major literary tradition to support him, nor even a faith among the people themselves that a Scottish literature is possible or desirable'. In this, Mr Muir is more or less summing up what has been said by nearly every modern Scots writer of importance, and shows in due course how Scott himself, in a moment of moving self-realisation, cried out against the historical material he dealt in, calling it 'stuffing my head with the most nonsensical trash'. Scott was so great a genius that what he dealt in must have some reality to the mind of living men. It is not that the history was untrue or was inadequate subject matter for his genius; it was that it no longer enriched or influenced a living national tradition; it had not even the potency of pure legend; it was story-telling or romance set in a void; it was seen backwards as in the round of some time spyglass and had interpretive bearing neither upon a present nor a future. Only some such intuition from Scott's 'secret world' could have drawn from him in his latter years these bitter words.

Mr Muir's great service to us here consists in analysing the meaning of this tradition; that is, he first isolates the elements that go to make a living tradition and then shows the inevitable result of their loss. Language, criticism, comparisons of Scottish poetry before and after the dissolution of Scots, the failure to achieve poetic drama, particular expressions of the Scots spirit as in Fantasy—each element is treated in turn with a fine precision. This section of the book is an original contribution of high value. The matter, however, is so condensed that an adequate résumé here is impossible. It may suffice for my purpose to indicate the trend of the discussion.

'The pre-requisite', writes Mr Muir, 'of an autonomous literature is a homogeneous language', Scotland had this language until 'sometime in the sixteenth century'. While it had it, it produced a literature that bore comparison with other national literatures; when it lost it, its literature decayed, because writers in Scotland were left not with one medium but with two: English for the expression of thought and Scots for the expression of emotion. Poetry of a major kind cannot be created by a mind thus divided. Great literature results from the fusion of thought and feeling on the highest plane. Where this fusion does not take place, poetry tends to become an irresponsible outburst of emotion and thought an arid expression of disapproval.

That Scotland had a homogeneous language, a single tongue for thought and emotion, up to the seventeenth century, we already know from the works of poets like Dunbar. How rich and varied the expression of this early period must have been, most of us are only beginning vaguely to realise. Mr Muir quotes an anonymous poem from the Bannatyne MS (1568) which he considers one of the supreme lyrics in Scottish literature. Its first lines evoked for me a memory of Donne's 'Ecstasy'. Yet it was written not only before the 'Ecstasy' but possibly long before Donne was born. He quotes other poems representing 'a quality in Scottish poetry which has been lost for good, a quality which has not been striven for since, even unsuccessfully'. He concludes this section with the sonnet by Mark Alexander Boyd (died 1601), which Mr Ezra Pound writes of as 'the most beautiful sonnet in English'. Altogether a remarkable period, of which we know only a few figures and 'a few scraps'. As Mr Muir points out, of the twenty-two poets Dunbar mentions in his 'Lament for the Makars', only four or five are known to us by their works.

It is supremely important that we realise not merely the richness and power and promise of this period, but its wholeness. These poets, writing in uninterrupted national tradition, were expressing the minds of a highly civilised society. Only when this is remembered may the disintegration that followed be understood. With this illuminating fact in his mind, Mr Muir has no great difficulty in resolving what Gregory Smith called 'The Caledonian Antisyzygy'. For all that it broadly amounts to is that we are back at the old division of mind again, with the opposites now labelled practical and fantastic, but with the critic attempting to reconcile the opposites by showing that the Scots poet can be at ease in 'both rooms of life' at the same time. Gregory Smith's analysis is brilliant and Mr Muir does it justice, but the truth surely is that you cannot be in both rooms at the same time; the best you can do is to hover in the doorway between, and however humorous, fantastic, and delightful may be your efforts at a double tenancy, the final result is 'a stationary disharmony, a standing frustration. For imagination and intellect do not reach a reconciliation in this poetry, but a comic deadlock.'

This lack of wholeness in the creative mind is seen in Burns and Scott and Stevenson. Mr Muir shows how in the one passage of 'Tam o' Shanter' where Burns 'makes a serious reflection on life' he drops into English. (The lines beginning: 'But pleasures are like poppies spread'.) 'It is clear that Burns felt he could not express it in Scots, which was to him a language for sentiment but not for thought.' In Scott, the division is still there, but—and one has to isolate this with more purpose than Mr Muir has done—it is not now so much a matter of language, for Scott could use English comprehensively, nor of the inhibiting force of Calvinism, for Scott was a Tory gentleman; it is a matter of the meeting place of all the dividing or opposing factors, in short, his environment, his country. After his first important work, the 'Minstrelsy of the Scottish Border', Scott said: 'Trivial as may appear such an offering to the Manes of a kingdom, once proud and independent, I hang it upon her altar with a mixture of feelings which I shall not attempt to describe.' Scott saw his country's 'manners and character ... daily melting and dissolving into those of her sister and ally'. And Mr Muir comments: 'By his collection of all sorts of relics and mementoes of Scotland's history ... he conceived concretely a broken image of the lost kingdom'. And that last poet's phrase sums up the whole matter. Scott's ordered legal thought was for the established order, for the Union; but his imagination, his vision, was with the broken image of the lost kingdom. The division we have been trying to grasp here reaches its final definition, and Mr Muir's last words are 'that he lived in a country which could not give an organic form to his genius'.

Now though Mr Muir, the literary critic, sees clearly that it is the inner secret knowledge of the loss of a kingdom, 'once proud and independent', that fatally divided Scott's genius, gathering up in its comprehensive truth all lesser considerations of nonsensical trash, of the personal feeling of being 'almost wholly neglected or left to myself', of religious manifestation and Fantasy, even of language itself; though he sees this not merely with a critic's acumen but with a poet's imagination, he yet fails when approaching the suasion or politics of his subject to apply this truth, the only one in the book which includes all opposites, all warring or disintegrating factors, and reconciles them.

The importance of this disability can hardly be overstressed, for it shows that the old division is still amongst us. In the sixteenth century, Scotland was a kingdom, and, for that age, had a great literature. Indeed, according to Mr Muir, 'the most sensitive and intelligent classes in Scotland were far more civilised four hundred years ago than they are now'. While still controlling her own destiny, Scotland was a country whose subjects had the innate power to make literature and to be highly civilised. The disruptive force was thus not native to the Scots character but brought from outside to bear upon it. Mr Muir's attempt, in this book and elsewhere, to find in the Reformation the major destructive force of the old native concord, is finally as unsatisfying as any of his other individual factors.

For what Mr Muir does not seem to see is that the 'rigours of Calvinism' were a symptom equally with other national phenomena like, for example, the rigours of the industrial revolution. England and Germany were reformed countries, yet their literary tradition continued and deepened. Ireland was never a reformed country, yet its ancient literary tradition disappeared with the loss of its nationhood. When Ireland once more fought for her nationhood and regained it, her literature reappeared (and in English, if with a difference) and Mr Muir uses names like Yeats and Joyce for critical conjuring on the highest plane. I am not concerned here with any argument for Scottish Nationalism. I am merely striving to find the principle which includes the facts and reconciles all opposites. The loss of nationhood does this. No other single factor or cause mentioned by Mr Muir does it.

If Mr Muir had faced up to this (as he does every now and then, and particularly in the case of Scott) and accepted all its implications, he would have saved us the last page of this book —surely one of the most signal instances of the Caledonian Antisyzygy run amok. 'I do not believe', he writes, 'in the programme of the Scottish Nationalists, for it goes against my reading of history, and seems to me a trivial response to a serious problem'. That can only mean that any deliberate action for the regaining of nationhood is trivial, for he immediately goes on: 'I can only conceive a free and independent Scotland coming to birth as the result of a general economic change in society, after which there would be no reason for England to exert compulsion on Scotland, and both nations could live in peace side by side'. In other words, we are to lie down under compulsion until other peoples bring about an economic change (whatever that may mean) which may permit a free and independent Scotland to be born. Is the idea, then, of a free and independent Scotland not 'trivial' after all? Apparently not, for Mr Muir at once proceeds: 'But meantime it is of living importance to Scotland that it should maintain and be able to assert its identity; it cannot do so unless it feels itself an entity; and it cannot feel itself an entity on a plane which has a right to human respect unless it can create an autonomous literature'. What do the words 'identity' and 'entity' mean here? Do they mean the nationhood of a free and independent Scotland, or do they mean some vague literary ideal to be perpetuated in a vacuum? How does a country *assert* its identity? And how, in particular, can the broken image of a lost kingdom 'create an autonomous literature' now, if it failed, as Mr Muir has so brilliantly shown, in the case of Scott, our greatest genius? But Mr Muir goes on: 'That sense of unity can be preserved by an act of faith, as it was preserved in Ireland'. Not economics now, but an act of faith! In Ireland, of course, they never troubled their heads about an economic change. They did not even bother about an act of faith; they simply acted with faith. But they *acted*. And their action was concerned solely with the restoration of nationhood. And Mr Muir holds them up as our example! Was ever unreason so varied within such short compass by so eminent a writer? But these obvious contradictions penetrate to an uneasy depth. For example, in his fine chapter on poetic drama, Mr Muir shows how the ancient national concord failed to go on to produce poetic drama, as other nations did whose tradition was not broken. If the essence of drama is conflict, how can there be drama, spiritual or physical, where the soul is prepared beforehand to refuse the issue? Yet here we have Mr Muir deliberately refusing the issue; suggesting that his country lie down to 'compulsion' until some other country or countries resolve the tragedy of its spiritual disharmony by providing for it a new way of distributing bread and butter.

It gives no pleasure to indulge in this sort of controversy. But it is important, I feel, that a writer who faces up to the absolutes in literary criticism should not hesitate over their implications when they are brought into the light of our common day. What was true in the case of Scott must apply surely with infinitely greater force to Mr Muir himself and to the Scottish writers of his time. If Mr Muir is certain in his mind that the dialectic of history has made consideration of Scottish nationhood 'trivial', then he would have been justified in asserting that as his expression of faith, and should have stopped there. But to have done that would have made of his book an antiquarian effort, a species of indulgence in 'nonsensical trash'. And Mr Muir—like the rest of us—knows it is too vital for that.

24

On Reviewing

Scots Magazine, 1941

A friend asked me the other day if I had noticed how extremely rare is a good review; in his opinion much rarer than a good book.

It is very difficult to discuss with fairness or balance such an opinion, because one's sympathy tends to be innately either with critic or creator. Critics have been thorns in the flesh of what is called the creative writer since writing began, and before the days of writing, poet or story-teller was no doubt pursued by his detractors.

That being said, the good review is rare, and probably has been in any age. If, in these days, it seems rarer than ever there may be reasons for it, such as lack of time. For example, not so long ago I read a review of a novel in which I was interested by a critic who in that same week reviewed eleven other novels. In his assessment of all twelve he was forthright and dogmatic. Now he may have been a fast worker, and the books he reviewed may not have been worth high consideration, but his criticism itself was self-evidently hurried and valueless. For by a good review I mean a review that satisfies the reader by evidence of insight, understanding, and judgement, that warms the reader's own understanding even when he has not read the book. Whether the book has been praised or condemned, in whole or in part, is beside the point, which here is solely the quality of the criticism.

Some six works of imagination for weekly assessment by a star reviewer has become the common order of popular criticism, and the reviewer is himself sometimes a practising novelist. Can the mind keep up its freshness under such an assault and battery by evoked emotions in 'tense moments' and 'thrilling situations'? Or does it go jaded and deal with human values according to some ready-made formula, much as we play an indifferent game of chess, or 'tell off' a detective story writer for not 'playing fair'? Take some of the most exquisite musical themes by the masters and have them mechanically reproduced at intervals to the sensitive ear, and in time the understanding behind the ear would surely go mad, if it could not protect itself by some formula of indifference.

One might think that if the reviewer did fall in with a really original work he would rejoice, he would thank his gods that here at last was something out of the deadly rut, something he could spread himself upon with an earnest cheer. But that is in fact rarely what happens. What most of us mean by an original work is something done along lines with which we are familiar and which we like, but with an unusual cleverness or distinction. But the work of a real original, like D H Lawrence, had something more to it than that; it had the quality of making many reviewers feel uncomfortable, for example, and so instead of praising they condemned it. I saw a review of a novel in an eminent weekly not long ago where the very clever and knowledgeable reviewer used the occasion to have a wallop at Lawrence. The poor fellow who was being reviewed was used, so to speak, as a peg from which to swing the wallop. From this, I got no impression whatsoever of the value of the book, and its author is a distinguished writer.

Now a certain amount of self-importance or egotism is understandable. Many reviewers are men who doubtless would have liked to have excelled in creative work themselves. It may (or may not) be that the quality of their work was too fine, too unusual, too original to find a publisher, and now, as reviewers, they have 'the awful bore' of reading and commenting upon inferior stuff and not unnaturally want to get a bit of their own back when the occasion warrants it. Who would blame them? But the result, unfortunately, is not a good review.

All reviewers, however, are not overworked. For the overworked I have respect and marvel often enough at their fresh approach and generosity. There are the reviewers who with time on their hands work to a theory of human affairs, and they are a different kettle of fish entirely. Mostly they are what is called highbrow, which means as a rule that they have not worked through their high theory to a final simplicity, to ultimate and catholic values. With anything operating outside the realm of their theory, they are impatient, and because of their sincere impatience, they cannot help passing judgement with an air of arrogance. This type of critic is usually concerned with the 'spirit of the age', and in the world of affairs has a distinct political alignment. To this critic the quality of the work remains important, but such importance is merely regretted if to him the 'direction' of the work is wrong. To-day this kind of criticism is very common, and indeed is rapidly becoming commonplace. A familiar instance of it is seen in the critic who spurns all 'bourgeois values' because they do not consciously shape in a Leftish direction.

Often, however, it is the writer who is sympathetic to this kind of critic who yet suffers most severely at his hands. The writer himself may have the Leftish theory strongly implanted in him, but creative work is different in kind from critical work, and is conditioned by the imagination rather than the intellect. The imagination has its own kind of prompting, its own truths and laws, and they are apprehended in a way that makes them more absolute than any ever-debateable criteria of the intellect. Take a simple instance of the Leftish conception of brotherhood. The critic tends to be concerned with the theory by which brotherhood may be attained, but the creative writer by the conception of brotherhood in being. Let us suppose that the creative writer has some knowledge of a society where man to man is, or has been, as a brother. He gives a picture of this society as best he can, with a wide range of human emotion in action and reaction. But he cannot import into this society what does not truly belong to it in order to help out a theory which both he and the critic may hold in our society to-day. In a fully functioning communal society, for instance, capitalism would not be a living issue, just as witch-burning is no longer a living issue in ours. The creative writer apprehends this intuitively and must remain true to his intuition. Whereupon the critic, concerned with the direction of our present-day society, becomes impatient and dismisses the work of the writer as bourgeois or primitive or irrelevant.

But to the writer himself his work is not irrelevant; it may indeed in his profounder depths appear supremely relevant, because he is concerned with what he apprehends as ultimate human values and the possibility of their free and fearless functioning. He sees, for example, theories of brotherhood today working through tentative practice to fear, lack of freedom, wholesale cruelty and death. He has read of it before in history, even in that originally supreme conception of brotherhood, the Christian religion. It was when Roman Catholic (in the Inquisition) and the Covenanter (consider the atrocities of Philliphaugh) had the theory of Christian brotherhood most dominant *in the intellect*, that they committed their worst sins against human brotherhood and were least Christian. Their theory for the propagation of Christ's church was unassailably logical. Destroy all heretics and there will be no heretics. But logic is only an affair of the intellect, and this is what the truly creative writer never forgets. He sees, so to speak, that to destroy heretics is not to destroy heretics but to create them. In our society to-day this kind of vision, this imaginative reason, is naturally not welcomed by the active theorists. It never was in any society. The creative writer has to reconcile himself to this and abide his critics; but it seems to me, if his vision is true, that writing of his, dealing with any kind of society, must have a very real bearing on his own society.

There is one other kind of critic which I might mention, if with some misgiving, for now we are entering the region of what has been called creative criticism. Here again, however, just as in the realm of social or political affairs, we find the theorist who has his own 'closed' system of ideas concerning art. To any creation outside that system he tends to be anti-pathetic. A cursory study of the reactions of some of our most distinguished living poet-critics to, say, a poet like Shelley illustrates in some measure what I mean; though here the matter may be additionally involved by the conscious holding of certain philosophic or religious views on the part of the critic. But without going so deeply into the matter as all that, we can see at once that the critic whose bias is purely intellectual will react adversely to the writer who deals with the evocation of living human emotion.

Living emotion to the intellectual is amorphous, without apparent shape or art-form, and he is rendered uncomfortable by it, much as a hostess with definite ideas on behaviour can be rendered uncomfortable by a non-conforming guest. So were (and still are) many critics made uncomfortable by D H Lawrence. This kind of critic cannot see the living moment, as it were, until it is dead; not until it is in the past can it for him assume a recognisable outline, a permanent form; not until then does it become suitable for art treatment.

Realist, idealist, sensualist—one might go on attempting to suggest closed systems of ideas and the critical criteria which proceed from them. But finally one would have to deal with the critic who is capable of producing the good review. What quality is it that operates in him over and above any particular system of ideas? As a first guess, I should say the rare quality of magnanimity. Magnanimity is not a simple quality of kindness; it is rather that light in the mind whereby the elements of what has been created are seen purely. Intention and the measure of achievement are thus apprehended and then expressed with a clarity of spirit free from idiosyncratic obscurity. The temper of this kind of criticism is such that not only is the casual reader aware of being enriched by a mutual understanding, but the writer of the book himself rises above any adverse criticism—if not at once then presently—because of the pleasure he finds in meeting one who appears to understand his ultimate intention. What was flawed may be made perfect in a future work, but meantime above all endeavour, and criticism of endeavour, is this fellowship of a mutual understanding in letters, and so in life itself. There is a proverb to the effect that to understand all is to forgive all. Perhaps in the light of a sufficiently fine magnanimity, to understand all is to give all.

25

The Novel at Home

Scots Magazine, 1946

This article was written originally for an American publication, *The Writer*, whose contributors dealt with a writer's problems.

Although I have written many books, I have never before offered a word of advice to a beginner; not, anyway, publicly like this. I have never myself asked anyone's advice, and I remember the slight shock I got when the first novel I wrote was accepted by a London publisher, and the publisher's reader, a distinguished literary man, made suggestions about certain phrases which I had used. For him these phrases were obviously condensed or intense to the point of obscurity. For me, they were no doubt a final form of clarity. I forget what I did about them—I suspect not much, but I feel pretty certain now that my critic was right: only, and this is the point—it has taken time and experience and some thought about the novel to make this admission a natural and pleasant one.

I doubt if any advice about the need for sincerity, integrity, simplicity, and so on is of much practical value to the beginner, simply because if he is young enough—and he usually is—these are the qualities which consume him: if not consciously then certainly in the form of eagerness and belief. Where belief, impulse, eagerness are lacking, he would be advised to tackle some other way of earning a livelihood. As a writer he just won't succeed. And I am not now considering the highest form of writing, the kind that remains as a perpetual possession, as literature. Whatever the level, the desire to write on that level must be genuine. It must be a desire, not a calculation. Given that, things can happen. It took all the different levels of writing through all time for Shakespeare to emerge.

Now I have been asked to write this article because an American critic said of my book *The Silver Darlings*, that it was 'written by one who lived in kinship with the matter of his writing', and accordingly it was thought I might have something to say about the apparent illusion by which this 'kinship' is produced. This is rather difficult to do, because it goes beyond any question of the mere facts. The novel deals with herring fishers on the northern coasts of Scotland, and I know about them because I was born and brought up there, went to sea in their boats, and mixed generally with all their ways of living. But 'kinship' or authenticity does not come from knowing the facts. Facts can be acquired easily enough. It comes rather from the attitude of the author to the facts. And this is the important thing.

For example, a writer could look upon simple fishermen carrying on their dangerous occupation upon some remote shore as primitives of an interesting kind. They might be for the literary world an unusual 'subject', treated in a certain grotesque or violent way, they might even provide a seasonal sensation in book production. But the novel so constructed would not have that final or residual element of 'kinship' or authenticity. That comes, I fancy, from something even deeper than a sympathetic effort at identity with the characters in the novel; possibly from nothing less than a profound respect for them, because they body forth the real men the writer knows—respect and the feeling that they have taught the writer something of the little he has learned about life. How they vary in character and situation is to him, then, of true dramatic significance. He is on a level with his subject, neither above it nor below it. It is more than big enough for him and he tries to do his best with it. His characters create themselves out of the life he knows. They come alive in his mind in their own right and have for him a true kinship.

One of the most mysterious things in writing is how this authenticity comes through to the reader. I know of a brilliant London author and critic who, because he needed money, thought he would have a shot at writing a popular or best-selling romance. Without belief in what he was doing, he yet did his utmost with all the vast ingenuity he possessed. The book, published, fell flat. Now though the simplest working girl could not tell what was wrong with it, she yet knew there was something wrong. She smelt as it were the false relationship of the creator to his puppets.

The heartening thing about all that is this. A novelist does not require to have a wide personal knowledge of the world. What he needs to know is his own region and what he has to be sure of is his own attitude towards it. If he simply feels superior to it and despises it, then he won't write even tolerable satire about it, for somewhere in satire love lies choked or thwarted. But if he genuinely feels that his home town or farm or factory is big enough for him and can be used to express the deepest that is in him, then from that moment his novel can assume a living form, and, if it has the power, will be able to travel through all the countries and cultures in the world.

That, however, is not the whole story. Though a novelist may not know intimately much beyond his own region or state, he will treat of it all the better if he has some real knowledge of what is going on in the different countries of the world. With this extra knowledge, however acquired, his writing will tend to lose a certain provincial note. He does not need to intrude this extra knowledge for a moment. To have it in his mind, even lying forgotten, is enough. To drag it in, however cleverly, is to show off, and we are all sensitive to bad manners.

Perhaps I could illustrate this in some measure by referring to a recent couple of novels of mine, for this is necessarily a very personal matter. Fellow craftsmen can but swop their experiences, leaving it to the professors to be didactic. Well, I wrote a novel about an old man and a little boy living quietly in the Highlands of Scotland (where I live myself). Nothing you would say, could be more removed from the world of war and political theory. No violence, no killings, only simple daily happenings, against a given back-ground and an old Gaelic culture. In a sense it would be difficult to produce anything more 'provincial', and apparently socially dying at that.

But that's not quite the way it struck me. We all follow political movements at home and abroad and argue about Socialism and Communism. But our arguments are necessarily hypothetical; our concept of the brotherhood of man is a theory in the head; realisation must be an affair of the future. Here in the Highlands of Scotland, however, we still have traces of that old Gaelic communal culture I have mentioned. Thinking over it, I began to understand what a true form of communal living might mean. I have thus had intimations of it from actual life. And a novelist must not only know things in the head like a theorist, or from observation like an anthropologist, but he must also know them in his blood. So knowing them, he can check up on the theorist or anthropologist. In short, the little incidents or happenings, the legends and ways of speech and action, the attitude to nature, of the old man and the little boy take on for me a certain significance which is not confined to a region or province. This, of course, may be my fond illusion. I cannot help that. Nor does it matter, so long as it is genuine to me, and, in particular, so long as I have in my writing told the truth (literal and aesthetic) and not been consciously influenced by propaganda.

I hope it is unnecessary for me to say that I am not making any claims for this book as a book. It may be a very bad book. The reader settles that for himself. But I am making the claim that a young novelist writing, say, about some lost area in the Middle West can give it universal significance. If he does not succeed, it's not his subject that lets him down, it's himself.

Let me take this contention a step further. Some of the readers of my book about the boy Art and the old man Hector wanted me to write more of their adventures. I refused, because I felt I had written enough of that kind of adventure. And just here the knowledge of what was happening in the world—we were still some way from the landing in France—began to infiltrate. The notion of testing, as it were, the ways of life of the old man and the little boy against the conscious ideology of totalitarianism got a grip on my mind that I couldn't shake off. In actual life we know perfectly well what would have happened; the two simple country folk would have been physically liquidated. But my concern here was not for the physical but for the mental, for that state of mind which produces the physical manifestation. The fundamental conflict is between states of mind. In essence my problem was spiritual, not physical. I knew a little about the Continent before the war. I had books published there. Now I tried to get all the information I could about what was happening inside the concentration camps of Europe. With an ever increasing sense of horror I began to perceive that the human mind could be conditioned, that Hitler's boast of a domination of Europe for a thousand years was a conceivable possibility. Nothing less was at stake, it seemed to me, than the overthrow of two thousand years of our western civilisation. I studied as far as I could the techniques whereby the adult mind could be broken down or conditioned and the young mind moulded. And I'm not now referring only to physical tortures, applied in their infinite and horrible variety, but, in the case of the highly civilised individual, to the subtle attacks upon the inner citadel of the mind by the expert psychologist.

But I need not enlarge on this. A novelist is concerned with the human mind and its values. At the end of the first book dealing with the old man and the little boy I left them heading for the river which the boy had always longed to see. At the beginning of the second book they reach the river, start poaching a salmon, fall through the bottom of a deep pool, and wake up in their Gaelic paradise, called the Green Isle of the Great Deep. This paradise is run on totalitarian lines, and so my problem is set.

But the problem for the novelist is not just to manipulate the clash of ideas or ideologies. His real business is to see how his two individuals in this new milieu naturally react. He can never depart far from them. When God appears he must in some measure be a projection of the old Highlander's highest thought or wisdom. For even into phantasy, the novelist must import some ultimate sense of reality.

Anyway I wrote the book. Intellectual critics said some nice things about it, possibly because it dealt, after its fashion, with ideas. But the interesting thing for us here is that no critic, so far as I know, said it was a poor story. The old man and the young boy were still having adventures. In a word, far from being 'provincial', the place back home can be turned into paradise and include in its talk the basic problems of a planet.

The only advice, then, I can offer to the aspiring novelist is to treat of what he knows with the attitude towards it which I have suggested. If my experience should provide some new impulse or hope, then I shall almost feel justified in having overcome an initial reluctance to write in this personal way.

26

Why I Write

Gangrel, 1951

Why do I write? I haven't the foggiest notion. The mind baulks before the personal question and puts up the shutters. But presently it saunters out round them prepared for a saving game of generalisation. One writes for the same reason as another makes boats or rockeries or horn spoons. Man likes making things. Where I was a small boy, a grown man gave his oath 'before my Maker'. The old Scots poets were called Makars. Why we—or the Makar—should want to make or create things is still to me, despite Pavlov's dogs and materialist psychology, pure mystery.

However, analysis is our game; perhaps a sublimation of the old hunting instinct whereby, in the absence of lions and tigers, antelopes and hares, we hunt atoms and souls through universes and jungles to their inmost lairs. Sex, power, money—there's a simple beginning: a fellow writes for money.

And the first money is bright, incredible. Contrasted with the weekly wage envelope or even the monthly cheque, it is fairy gold, to be thrown abroad as a tree throws its leaves. It equates the act of making, which has been filched from the wage envelope. This is luck. From the essay or short story to a novel. The novel is a Book Society Choice. The golden leaves fall as in Vallombrosa. You walk in at the door of the house you got other makers to build on credit and call it your own. Miracle. And now, besides, there's another book.

But this time, alas, your helpful and courteous publishers look glum. They are prepared to publish, but … And in a flash you see that if you persist in this course—when you could pursue the earlier one—there are to be no more golden leaves; worse, the 'promising' tree itself will be publicly axed; worse still, you are aware it is not much of a book, perhaps even a bad book. Yet you persist, smiling, pig-headed, incomprehensible. And in due course the publishers' dire prognostications are fulfilled. Actually in the old legend the fairy gold when brought to the light of common day turned into horse dung. And you think to yourself: my God, how did these primitive myth-makers know about money and publishing?

Then a really astonishing thing happens. Something—probably that primitive snake in the grass—grins. *You were nearly had*, he says, *but now you're free* again. And you can pelt him with the sourest grapes you can lay your hands on. It makes no difference. He enters into fathomless conspiracy with you. His arabesques glitter with laughter in the sun.

Meantime that word primitive has put me on the spoor of something (which is why I write). A book on field anthropology—*Sex and Temperament* by Margaret Mead—slips into mind. I remember her admirable description of a poor hill tribe in New Guinea (which the Japs were so occidentally anxious to civilize). They lived in a truly communal way and got the greatest fun from cultivating one another's gardens. A gentle affectionate laughing people who could not understand violence. For certain purposes, however, they needed a 'big man', a leader or fuhrer. So they caught young what looked a likely lad and got him to shout ersatz insults at his opposite number from across the valley. A real Hitler or Mussolini at his declamatory best would have burst into fragments upon their awe and/or laughter. Even their own fuhrer when fully trained remains uncorrupted by power, waiting for the day when he may retire and laugh happily ever after. The day is achieved in the time dimension when his eldest child reaches puberty. So, as we say, it was up to him to get cracking on the sex business.

Primitives, of course. No conception of Progress. But from this aspect of their culture pattern, does no echo of the laugh come through to us? Would a wise old Chinaman smile? A Yogi contemplate? A Christian saint or mystic understand? Where does Marx come in? And the psychoanalysts?

Success, money, Fuhrer, horse dung. Odd notions and contrasts begin to trouble the writer. He is aware that for some inexplicable reason raw material is starting to collect. Arguments like elvers tie knots on their own tails. He even hears beforehand critical jibes about his searching back through diffusionist theories to a Golden Age, a Garden of Eden. But he doesn't worry, for at least he knows a lot about culture patterns; and is primarily concerned with his own amazing one here to-day—and perhaps to-morrow.

And now from everywhere—work, politics, economics, parties, committees an' all—material of a raw relevancy flows fatally in; until the whole thing is a morass mocked by a will o' the wisp, an elusive glimmer of light, for which he has no lantern. No fable. No conceivable book. How superbly lucky are the fellows who get wage envelopes! Up go the shutters. And then one day—only heaven knows how or why—he observes his unfortunate hand beginning to make scrawls on the mud of the morass with a crooked stick.

And then again—for he realises now that it is all pure mystery to his bloody cost—he makes the astounding discovery that what the stick is designing has apparently nothing whatever to do with success, tribes in New Guinea, fuhrers, or Gardens of Eden. Instead, here are fellows sailing a boat, or working at a beach; or a girl tranced by a singing blackbird while she is thinking of something else.

Man emerging from the sucking morass to sing again with a vivid spontaneity of the spirit. … Is that the hidden notion of it all? Or what? And he must be careful (his own culture pattern being what it is) to slaughter the poetry in his prose. Off stage a monotonous Indian voice is intoning: All is a striving and a striving and an ending in nothing. How profoundly right the fellow is! Comforted, you irrationally get hold of the stick again. To hell with poverty, let us kill a hen. You began to write.

Afterword

Belief in Ourselves, the title chosen for this collection of essays by Neil M Gunn, one of Scotland's greatest 20th century novelists, reflects the author's keen interest in the social and political realities of the Scotland in which he lived. The sister collection of essays, *Landscape to Light*, published in 2009, can be understood as a spiritual pilgrimage in which the emphasis is placed on a hunt for enlightenment on a personal level. *Belief in Ourselves* is firmly rooted in the social aspects of living and working together for the good of the community without any loss of individual freedom. This idea of community from the level of parish to that of nation had a particular relevance during the period in which the author lived and wrote. That period spanned the Depression, the political and financial crises of the 1930s, the emergence of totalitarian regimes in Germany, Italy, Spain and Soviet Russia and the Second World War and its depressing aftermath. Although the backdrop he uses for most of his novels and essays is that of the Highlands of Scotland, the thrust of his writing is of a universal nature and underlines his fundamental belief that to understand other cultures, one has to know one's own. In the context of these essays the concept of nationalism extends to encompass thoughts on co-operation on land and sea, the value of tradition and the vital role played by literature in engendering feelings of national identity and personal freedom in a world that was witnessing the frightening uniformity of totalitarianism and the subtle levelling by a bland form of cosmopolitism. The essays are not presented in chronological order but rather by theme.

The Caithness community into which Gunn was born in 1891 was warm and friendly and traditionally Highland. His father, a fishing boat skipper, enjoyed the reputation of being both adventurous and successful. Fishing, however, was in decline, and none of the seven boys in his family followed his father to sea. Three emigrated to Canada and four (including Neil Gunn) took up careers in the Civil Service and teaching. As a boy of obvious brilliance and ability, Gunn was to leave his local school to pursue his education at the hands of a private tutor employed by an elder sister and her doctor husband in Kirkcudbrightshire in the South West of Scotland. From there Gunn entered the Civil Service and worked both in London and Edinburgh before qualifying as an officer in the Customs and Excise Service. His career was interrupted by the First World War, but the work in which he was involved for the Admiralty kept him in the Highlands, where he was to remain for the rest of his life.

Although his early literary life as a writer of poetry, essays and short stories began during the First World War, he became a much more mature and accomplished writer in the 1920's. The stimulus for this was largely his reaction to the Caithness he found on his return there as a fully fledged excise officer in 1922. He saw the county he had known and loved as a child in steep economic decline. His first novel, *The Grey Coast* (1926) and his essay *Defensio Scotorum* (1928) reflect his feelings of despair. In the essay he writes, '45 per cent of us live more than two in a room; we have the highest death rate, sick rate, infant mortality rate, emigration and immigration rate in the British Isles.' Such a well worn cliché as 'Scotland: my auld respected mither' just would not do. He saw the way ahead for the necessary changes through Scottish independence. The consequences of this huge political step would be profound: the process of social and economic decline would be arrested; Scotland would emerge once again as one of the main contributors to European culture and Scottish individuality would be seen with such truth of vision, such certainty in delineation, excusing nothing, distorting nothing. He concluded that in the last analysis the basic trouble afflicting Scotland was a politico-economic one. The essay anticipated the writing of Gunn's most bitter novel *The Lost Glen* (1932), in which he portrays the dire economic situation of the crofting and fishing communities in the Highlands and the demeaning aspect of the work undertaken by them to cater for the needs of the fishing and shooting fraternity of landowners and wealthy visitors.

The bleak but realistic portrayal of the subject matter in these early works was more than ample proof that Gunn had dispensed with any vestiges of the seductive influence of the Celtic Twilight movement with its beautiful pessimism concerning a dying culture. *Morning Tide* (1931), a novel written after *The Lost Glen*, but published before it, was more than an idyll of childhood spent in a northern community; it reflected Gunn's conviction that there was something in the psyche of the local people in his native parish that could restore belief in themselves and encourage them to move forward in different ways. .

In 1929 Gunn joined the National Party of Scotland and over the following years was instrumental in effecting its eventual merger with the Scottish Party to form the Scottish National Party. In 1931 he campaigned for John McCormick as the candidate for the National Party of Scotland in the Parliamentary election of that year. During these exciting years of political manoeuvring and high hopes for some form of Home Rule, Gunn's home in Inverness was considered by many to be the ideological headquarters of the emerging party. Gunn was a clear thinker as for him the aim was obvious and simple: a Scottish Parliament with fiscal control and with authority to determine the nation's future constitution and political status. Because of his employment in the Civil Service, Gunn's work on the political scene had to be confined to participating in discussions, writing brochures and articles, drafting documents of political import and quiet diplomacy. It was not until after the success of his novel *Highland River* (1937), the winner of the prestigious James Tait Black Memorial prize, that Gunn was unfettered from all constraints and able to resign from the Civil Service and become a full-time writer. He decided to leave Inverness with its vibrant social and political life and seek the comparative seclusion of a farm house in the hill country near Dingwall, the county town of Ross and Cromarty, to find the necessary peace to pursue his literary endeavours. There he was to experience the most prolific time of his creative life, writing 11 novels in the space of 11 years; the temptation was there to devote his energies to fiction coloured by matters of the spirit and the wonder of nature. But the War made it impossible for him to remain isolated from outside events. He supported the War effort and maintained his interest in the work of the Scottish National Party.

As far back as 1931 in an essay entitled *Nationalism and Internationalism* he had elucidated his thoughts on nationalism within the context of world politics. At a time when words like nationalism and even patriotism could be misconstrued by those who believed in a bland form of liberal democracy, Gunn had to be forthright in portraying his understanding of these words. He writes, 'Nationalism creates that which internationalism enjoys. The more varied and multiple your nationalism, the richer and profounder your internationalism.' He saw the small state as humanity's last bulwark for personal expression against impersonal tyranny, for the quick freedom of the spirit against the flattening steamroller of mass. The same argument permeated his idea of patriotism, which he saw as a force based on tradition. 'And it is only when a man is moved by the traditions and music and poetry of his own land that he is a position to comprehend those of any other land for he has already the eyes of sympathy and ears of understanding.' Later in that decade and during the Second World War the word nationalism had been tainted by its appropriation by the 'National' Socialists in Germany, better known as the Nazis. For many, including Gunn, the enemies in the War were not the Germans themselves but rather those who had espoused the cause of national socialism. To further their aims the Nazis pursued a policy of discovering and influencing possible sympathisers or fellow travellers elsewhere in (Ayran) Europe. Gunn's work was known in Germany. *Morning Tide* had been translated into German by a certain Fritz Wolcken, and published in Munich in 1938. Gunn maintained a friendly relationship with Wolcken, whom he regarded as a good German. Indeed Wolcken showed his deep interest in Gunn's oeuvre by starting the translation of the anti-utopian *Green Isle of the Great Deep* (1944) whilst in a British prisoner-of-war camp. It was *Butcher's Broom* (1934), Gunn's novel of the Clearances,that attracted the attention of those seeking something compatible with Nazi views on race. In the novel Gunn was using the forms of reference of the time, particularly the idea of race. Indeed, in a BBC broadcast in 1929[1] he claimed that the Scottish novelist Neil Munro stood for the Gaelic spirit which was the essential spirit at the back of the Scottish race. This theme is explored and enlarged in the essays *The Hidden Heart* (1928) and *The Gael will come again* (1931). There were rumours emanating from Germany that *Butcher's Broom* was a candidate for the award of the Shakespeare prize from the University of Hamburg, given annually to those who had contributed in some significant way to the 'Nordic ideal'. It was a strange choice as that novel was positively against any form of totalitarianism. In this confused period of European history propaganda from both Germany and Russia – especially from Russia – could be persuasive and misleading. In its early days the Soviet experiment evoked a considerable amount of sympathy among the intellectual Left in the West as shown in *Scotland a Nation* (1936), and perhaps rightly so from what was believed to be the truth. Such sentiment was strengthened at the time of the Soviet Union's entry into the War as an important ally. In his essay *The Essence of Nationalism* (1942) Gunn gives credit to Stalin for encouraging non-Russian nationalities in terms of preserving their culture and language at a time when the dictator was moving whole peoples from their homelands to vast spaces of Siberia. Gunn would have been horrified if he had known this as he believed in the fundamental desire for people to have their own land where they could be allowed to labour and produce in peace. In poetic language he extols the virtue of attachment to a piece of land. 'To love your own land, from which you draw your deepest inspiration is as natural as to love the sunlight or a woman, is to understand what moves in the heart of a Pole or Czech, is to salute Sibelius not in envy or hate but in admiration and gratitude.'

In 1940 he wrote his most definitive essay on nationalism, *Why are writers nationalists*. He begins by quoting from the spiritual autobiography of the distinguished poet and critic, Edwin Muir. This quote from *The Story and the Fable* encapsulates Gunn's essential beliefs on nationalism:

> 'Because of this I believe that men are capable of organising themselves only in relatively small communities,and that even then they need custom, tradition and memory to guide them. For these reasons I believe in Scottish Nationalism, and should like to see Scotland a self-governing nation. In great empires the quality of the individual life declines: it becomes plain and commonplace. The little tribal community of Israel, the city state of Athens, the relatively small England of Elizabeth's time, mean more in the history of civilisation than the British Empire. I am for small nations as against large ones, because I am for a kind of society where men have some real practical control of their lives. I am for a Scottish nation because I am a Scotsman.'

Gunn applauds this and from it develops the theme of the importance of tradition. He sees tradition as respect for and belief in the past that act as a source of creativity and encouragement for people in the present.

In supporting the War effort in the 1940s Gunn appreciated the need for a certain amount of collective activity in harnessing the potential of the country in its struggle for survival. This, at first sight, seemed at variance with the importance of individual freedom in which Gunn so passionately believed. But Gunn had already solved this problem in his writing in the 1930's by underlining the spirit of co-operation typical of the community of his childhood. Hardships beyond the capability of the individual to mitigate became the responsibility of the community at large.[2] The community was self sufficient; it owed much of this to its isolation, but that isolation did not in turn lead to insularity. Through its emigrants, its sailors, and its soldiers, the community was aware of the outside world, and, accordingly, the strength of its own values. In *The Atom of Delight* (1956), Gunn's spiritual autobiography, he postulates that these values may have grown out of the clan system, with its devotion, mutual trust and social warmth. Despite the betrayal of the clansfolk in the Clearances by their chiefs, the spirit of co-operation survived among the people themselves. It was a way of life, based on the inter-action of individual independence and mutual co-operation. The community ensured that the needs of the widow and the sick were met; it came together for peat cutting whilst preserving the individual's right to a particular peat bank. Although all this could be summed up as wistful thinking of times gone by, Gunn maintained that the spirit of co-operation remained within the Highland psyche and only needed some form of stimulus to translate it into meaningful economic activity. It is little wonder that in *A Visitor from Denmark* (1937) he admired the success of the Danes in using the principle of co-operation to good effect. Here was a country smaller than Scotland that had overcome cultural and economic incursions from bigger countries to fashion an industry and a culture that was essentially Danish. This was achieved by enlightened leadership at the right time. Gunn bemoans the fact that many of Scotland's finest leaders make their name in London or within the Empire. Would they have made their exit as quickly if there had been posts available in Scotland commensurate with their talents? – a point made in ...*and then rebuild it* (1939). This drain of natural leaders had not been helped by the attitude of many in authority who lacked belief in the Highlands and considered the only option for that huge area was to be a tourist attraction or a sporting reserve. Those who had not left to make their fortune or realise their potential elsewhere remained in a state of apathy, if not despair,

If Gunn in the 1930s is in despair over the state of farming and crofting, then that feeling of depression was even more marked in his assessment of the dramatic decline of the fishing industry. Gunn had obviously fond memories of his father and his exploits at sea against a background of a vibrant fishing community ashore. Gunn's great novel of the fishing boom of the early 19th century, *The Silver Darlings*,(1941) is dedicated to his father. Nothing could be more disheartening or depressing than viewing silted-up harbours, derelict boats, and boarded-up fishing stores and cooperages. Such sights were a common feature of the Caithness of the 1930's. In an angry essay *Sea and Land – and Finance* (1930) written under his pseudonym Dane McNeil he berates unthinking and unenlightened capitalists for the evils inflicted on the people who had depended on the sea and had brought life and warmth to the communities in which they lived. The Church too comes in for his invective for its passive acceptance of events that were in themselves against the interests and inherent beliefs of its parishioners. There is less emotion but the same theme in *The Fishermen of the North East* (1938), which provides a more comprehensive view of the great decline. In *The Family Boat* (1937) Gunn paints the most moving and human picture of those Scottish fishermen who jointly own the boat in which they sail. They still exist and are called 'share fishermen' as each has a share in the boat. Usually the skipper has 50% of the shares with the remainder being equally divided among the others (usually four in number). Even the legal term of 'joint adventurers' for this unusual partnership has a touch of panache and glamour about it. Alas, the number of share fishermen was on the decline; lack of finance made this form of co-operation difficult when times were hard, and there was not enough reserve capital to cope with the lean years. Those supported by the finance of off-shore investors in syndicates could better survive the bad times. In the same essay Gunn makes the very important point that the fishing industry is more important in Scotland than in England. (Recent figures [2000] show that 60% of the fish landed in the British Isles come through Scottish ports.) For Scotland, fishing was such an important industry and way of life that it called for local (national) control. Again Gunn looks to co-operation among share fishermen as a way of enabling them to compete with larger and better financed fishing syndicates. In an essay *A Footnote on Co-operation* (1968) written almost thirty years later Gunn makes the same point, and as forcibly.

Although in the essays of the 1930s the picture Gunn paints of the primary industries of Scotland is bleak, he rarely excludes a hope or recommendation for some form of revival or change of attitude. In *Scotland Moves* (1943) he writes of an exciting development emanating from a decision by the then Secretary of State for Scotland to introduce a bill, the Hydro-Electric Bill, to harness the immense potential of water power within Scotland. What pleased him was that the Bill had no connection with charity or dole but was a fully fledged business proposition that would pay for itself. It would also be of benefit not only to the Highlands alone but also to the country as a whole. For Gunn this 'change in the mental weather' of the Highlands could only bring back a sense of pride and confidence to the Highlanders themselves. It would be a source of employment for the soldiers returning from the War and an encouragement for them to remain in a country that offered them a future. What was more important for Gunn was that this would be a venture pursued in Scotland by Scotsmen themselves for the benefit of a wider community. *Belief in Ourselves* (1945) continues with his theme of the reconstruction of the Highlands and dwells on a success story of the sheepfarming clubs and the urgent need for the formation of co-operatives of share fishermen to harness their economic potential in an increasingly competitive section of the economy. He sees a healthy economy as an essential ingredient in the restoration of the Highlanders' belief in themselves. He writes, 'In all this there is one thing that particularly interests me, and that is that I should like to see the new energy and impetus provided by Highlanders themselves, by those who derive from the old traditions, so that what was fine in our culture, our ways of life and our behaviour, might continue.'

In all his thinking Gunn saw economic health and culture as being closely intertwined. Both were constituent parts of a healthy nation. As a writer he was actively involved in a resurgence of Scottish culture in a movement that came to be called 'The Scottish Renaissance'. In an early essay *New Golden Age for Scottish Letters* (1930) he is anxious to redefine 'Renaissance' as being more of a National Awakening rather than simply a rebirth of the arts on the lines of the Italian Renaissance, without necessarily having a sprinkling of people of genius. What was important for him were not the attractions and stimulus of genius but rather the bringing to birth once more of a Scottish culture on a national scale. Past failures of Scots enterprise, in whatever field, had been due to the lack of a sustaining culture; too many individuals had had no faith in, had not been profoundly conscious of, their life-giving roots. In a further article written three years on *The Scottish Renascence* (1933) Gunn reasserts the unrestricted nature of the movement. 'Altogether let it be emphasised that renascence does not necessarily imply or demand the emergence of one or more great figures … but rather a reawakening or rebirth amongst many people, ultimately discernible even in the minor social manifestations of a whole people.' His point is simply that the appropriate conditions must first be created within a nation for individual genius to emerge and thrive.

As late as 1962 in an essay *The Scottish Renaissance* Gunn had to counter the established view that Hugh MacDiarmid was the Scottish Literary Renaissance. Whilst he acknowledges that such a view is understandable because of the high profile of MacDiarmid, he considers the simple equation of man and movement to be an exaggeration and even a denial of the true situation as MacDiarmid himself saw it then. 'Indeed his (MacDiarmid's) articles and editings would have been pointless unless there had been in Scotland sufficient activity and accomplishment in cultural affairs to warrant his use of a word like Renaissance.' Although two very distinguished writers, Grassic Gibbon and Edwin Muir, had chosen a position outside the movement, the movement itself, underpinned by its political ideas and beliefs, had held its ground.

In a interesting and revealing essay *Literature: Class or National* (1936) Gunn refuted the argument that literature originated in social class and that class solidarity could be a force for the creation of working class art. The originator of the article to which Gunn was responding claimed that literature was dominated by the middle classes who provided nationalism as a distracting escape from the class struggle. In his measured response Gunn uses the work of Grassic Gibbon as an example of the importance of seeking inspiration from one's roots. That writer's imagination throve when it came to deal with Scotland but remained moribund in his non-Scottish work. Grassic Gibbon had to come back to his own country, his own people before what had moved him so deeply received it profoundest expression. Yet that did not blind him to the social inequalities and injustices within Scotland itself. Like Grassic Gibbon, Gunn was acutely conscious of the flaws and warts of Scottish society and wished to erase them, but, unlike Grassic Gibbon, he rejected Marxism as the moving force to lead to the imminent regeneration of Scotland. Gunn also looked forward to a vital working class literature, one which, in terms reminiscent of T S Eliot on tradition, would not be divorced from past expressions of art, but on the contrary, would be added to them, affecting them all by its presence, as it (and they) would be affected in turn by the art of a later age.

In his essay *Nationalism in Writing – Tradition and Magic* (1938) Gunn returns to the work of Grasssic Gibbon and pays tribute to him as great and imaginative author – albeit one who chose not to be identified with the Scottish Renaissance. Gunn deftly divides his subject into the idealist who wishes at all costs to remove cruelty, injustice and human deprivation from the world, even if that meant being overrun by an alien power, and the supremely creative artist who so obviously derived his strength and inspiration from his native Mearns. Gibbon looked back to an age before history, before the human story had become contaminated by civilisation – a sort of golden age. The outcome of his most famous book, *Sunset Song* (1932) may be depressing but the delight the writer manages to communicate in his character creation and descriptive narrative is described by Gunn as the stuff of magic. Gunn writes, 'I maintain that the delight he communicates is something beyond this; beyond the narration of seedtime and harvest in earth and brute; beyond a last human concern for the girl Chris Guthrie even; it is the transfusing spirit or essence of these and all that goes to give them substance and texture in a living and eternal pattern, and it is evoked by what I can only think of at the moment as incantation.'

In *Nationalism in Writing II – The Theatre Society* (1938) Gunn writes, 'Associations or parties, aiming at the freedom of the body politic, have been more strongly at work, have received greater publicity and have been better organised than any associations working for a cultural expression. I do not say that they have been more important, for body and mind make a single working unit and neither can function without the other.' Again, Gunn stresses the need for cultural bodies such as a national theatre, through which writers could express the nation's essential self. Indeed, writers needed the context of independence to provide them with the freedom for individual creation. In his view there could be no vital culture without a correspondingly strong sense of political identity.

In *Nationalism in Writing III – Is Scottish Individualism to be deplored?* (1939) Gunn returns to the complementary relationship between economy and culture in the creation of a strong and confident nation. Scotland could boast of a long and distinguished tradition of democratic development visible in the Declaration of Arbroath in 1320 and lived in the clan system in the Highlands. Scotland's church and legal systems grew out of this and were admired throughout the world. Its economy, however, had not kept pace with these social developments and the way ahead was for more collaboration and co-operation in all sectors of economic activity. The paradox of co-operation was that economic strength could be obtained without any loss in individual freedom. Gunn wonders why the Scot should have retained his or her individualism but lost the capacity for economic co-operation. He poses the question, 'Does the logical answer lie in the possibility that the Scot was inevitably doomed to lose his capacity for co-operation from the very moment that he abdicated his power to deal with his own economic relations?'

In *Review of Scott and Scotland* (1936) Gunn turns his attention to the book written by a man for whom he had great admiration both as critic and poet, Edwin Muir. The book was one of The Voice of Scotland series published by Routledge for which Gunn had written about the significance of whisky in the culture of the country in *Whisky in Scotland* (1935). Although Gunn admired the lucid explanation given by Muir over the dilemma facing Scott over the language problem of feeling in Scots and thinking in English, he did not agree with all Muir's analyses of the cause of Scotland's lack of a literature comparable to that of England and Ireland. (Muir had placed much of the blame on the stultifying effect of Calvinism from the 16th century onwards and that the Bible was read using the King James Version with its exquisite English prose.) Muir could only conceive a free and independent Scotland with an autonomous culture coming to birth as the result of a general economic change in society, after which the influence of England in all spheres would diminish. Gunn saw the independence of Scotland as a prerequisite for the emergence of a national literature and a feeling of self belief so necessary for a vibrant culture. Above all, an act of faith was called for.

Gunn's undisguised admiration of Muir as a discerning and well informed critic comes through in general terms in a later essay, *On Reviewing* (1941). Gunn considers a good review as valuable as a good book. The thoughtful reviewer has his duty towards not only the reading public but also the writer of the book reviewed. With regard to his own books, Gunn knew when the reviewer had truly grasped the essential elements in the work, had identified the heart of the matter. He became a sort of companion, whose views could be helpful in the long run, even if they were at variance with his own. Gunn took his writing seriously and although financial success was obviously important to him, he was always conscious of his responsibility of providing his readership with thoughts that were worth pondering. He is at his most revealing in an essay for American readership on his kinship with his created characters. In *The Novel at Home* (1946) he makes it clear that he never feels superior to the characters he describes no matter how humble their station in life may be. The simplest character could be the most illuminating in terms of thought and action. The people about whom he wrote were based on his experience of them and what could be derived from them could be of universal import. He gave as an example the story of the dialogue between an old man and a young boy in *Young Art and Old Hector* (1942) a timeless dialogue. He made the same characters his protagonists in a totalitarian state in *The Green Isle of the Great Deep* (1944). Their traditional wisdom opposed to the crushing conformity of the state. This idea of the universal significance of simple things and the enlightened use of the inductive process were to be found in most of his novels.

In the final essay *Why I Write* (1951) Gunn expresses delight in the art of 'making' or creating, the ups and downs of dealing with publishers, the morass of raw material from which to draw for his work and the mystery of dealing with himself. Gunn had several works to write after that essay had been written, including his own spiritual autobiography *The Atom of Delight* (1956). Gunn believed intensely in the value of experience and felt that he could talk and write with authority about the primary activities of crofting and fishing in the Highlands. This was recognised in the 1950's when he was invited to join a Commission of Enquiry into Crofting Conditions. Gunn found the experience both enjoyable and satisfying. He was more than satisfied with the final report. It begins with a statement of the premise upon which it is based, that is that 'crofting as a way of life should be maintained' and later, 'we have thought it right … to record our unanimous conviction, founded on personal knowledge and on the evidence received, that in the national interest the maintenance of these communities is desirable, because they embody a free and independent way of life which in a civilisation predominantly urban and industrial in character is worth preserving for its own intrinsic quality.' Throughout the Report the preservation of the culture and tradition of the crofters is emphasised and this emphasis is usually accompanied by a corresponding stress upon co-operation and self-help. It is not difficult to see the imprint of Gunn on this positive and encouraging document.

Before his death in 1973 Gunn was to see the emergence of a new Crofters Commission (1955) and the founding of the Highlands and Islands Development Board; he campaigned for the creation of a Highland university, a dream that was to be realised after his death. His efforts by the pen reflecting political beliefs derived from his own Highland background did much to arrest the cultural, social and economic decline of Scotland, and the Highlands in particular. His considerable literary talents were recognised in 1972 by the award of a fellowship in his name for distinguished foreign writers. This was a fitting honour for a writer who regarded belief in his own country in all its aspects as the best way to understand the value of the culture of other countries and to forge friendships that transcended national boundaries.

While the essays in this collection are very much situated in their time, their themes are ageless and hold a strong relevance to today's world. The relationship between the individual and his community mirrors that between the writer and his readership. The interaction of the individual and the artist towards their communities is an essential component in the shaping of a nation and its traditions.

---

1   BBC Talk, Scotland Today Series, 'Scottish Letters', February, 1929.

2   Gunn was also aware of Prince Kropotkin's theories of 'mutual aid' and the ideas of anarchism. He wrote to Naomi Mitchison in 1944: 'And when you accuse me of anarchism, do you mean the anarchism of Kropotkin or individual chaos? There's a mighty difference.' *Neil M gunn, A Highland Life* by F R Hart & J B Pick, London: John Murray, 1981. p 180. He wrote also to Margaret McEwan: 'I was always an anarchist.' Ibid.

Sources and Further Reading

Sources

Why are Writers Nationalists?, Stirling: *The Scots Independent*, November 1940, No. 162, p. 7

The Essence of Nationalism, Dundee: *The Scots Magazine*, June 1942, Vol. 37, No. 3, pp. 169–172

Nationalism and Internationalism, Dundee: *The Scots Magazine*, June 1931, Vol. 15, No. 3, pp. 185–188

Defensio Scotorum, (by Dane McNeil), Dundee: *The Scots Magazine*, April 1928, Vol. 9, No. 1, pp. 51–58

The Hidden Heart, (by Dane McNeil), Dundee: *The Scots Magazine*, August 1928, Vol. 9, No. 5, pp. 331–335

Scotland a Nation, *Left Review*, November 1936, London, Vol 2, No 14, pp. 735–738

The Gael Will Come Again, (by Dane McNeil), Dundee: *The Scots Magazine*, February 1931, Vol. 14, No. 5, pp. 324–327

A Visitor from Denmark, Dundee: *The Scots Magazine*, May 1937, Vol. 27, No. 1, pp. 96–101

A Footnote on Co-operation, London: *Anarchy* 86, April 1968, Vol. 8, No. 4, pp. 116–117

The Family Boat, Dundee: *The Scots Magazine*, June 1937, Vo. 27 No. 3, pp. 169-74

Sea and Land – And Finance – The Church's great silence, (by Dane M'Neil), *The Healing of the Nation: The Scottish Church and a waiting people – A symposium*. Ed. Rev. J. W. Stevenson, T & T Clark, Edinburgh, 1930, pp. 81–82

The Fishermen of the North East, Glasgow: *Scotland*, Autumn 1938, Vol 3, No 3, pp. 13–16

... and then rebuild it, Dundee: *The Scots Magazine*, December 1939, Vol. 32, No. 3, pp. 173–178

Scotland Moves, Dundee: *The Scots Magazine*, September 1943, Vol. 39, No. 6, pp. 447–450

Belief in Ourselves, Dundee: *The Scots Magazine*, September 1945, Vol. 43, No. 6, pp. 424–427

New Golden Age for Scots Letters, Glasgow: *Daily Record*, 28th. May 1930, No. 26004, p. 5

The Scottish Renaissance, Dundee: *The Scots Magazine*, June 1933, Vol. 19, No. 3, pp. 201–204

Literature: Class or National?, Edinburgh: *Outlook*, July 1936, Vol. 1, No. 4, pp. 54–58

Nationalism in Writing I – Tradition and Magic in the Work of Lewis Grassic Gibbon, Dundee: *The Scots Magazine*, October 1938, Vol. 30, No. 1, pp. 28–35

Nationalism in Writing II – The Theatre Society of Scotland, Dundee: *The Scots Magazine*, December 1938, Vol. 30, No. 3, pp. 194–198

Nationalism in Writing III – Is Scottish Individualism to be Deplored, Dundee: *The Scots Magazine*, July 1939, Vol. 31, No. 4, pp. 275–282

Scottish Renaissance, Glasgow: *Scottish Field*, August 1962, Vol. 109, No. 716, p. 34

Review of Scott and Scotland Scott, Dundee: *The Scots Magazine*, October 1936, pp. 72–78

On Reviewing, Dundee: *The Scots Magazine*, August 1941, Vol. 35, No. 5, pp. 364–36
The Novel at Home, Dundee: *The Scots Magazine*, April 1946, Vol. 45, No. 1, pp. 1–5
Why I Write, London: *Gangrel*, Summer 1946, No. 4, pp. 10–11

Major Writings

The Grey Coast – London: Jonathan Cape, 1926
Hidden Doors (Short stories) – Edinburgh: The Porpoise Press, 1929
Morning Tide – Edinburgh: The Porpoise Press, 1931
The Lost Glen – Edinburgh: The Porpoise Press, 1932
Sun Circle – Edinburgh: The Porpoise Press, 1933
Butcher's Broom – Edinburgh: The Porpoise Press, 1934
Whisky & Scotland: A Practical and Spiritual Survey (History) – London: George Routledge & Sons, 1935
Highland River – Edinburgh: The Porpoise Press, 1937
Off in a Boat (Travel) – Edinburgh: The Porpoise Press, 1938
Wild Geese Overhead – London: Faber & Faber, 1939
Second Sight – London: Faber & Faber, 1940
The Silver Darlings – London: Faber & Faber, 1941
Young Art and Old Hector – London: Faber & Faber, 1942
Storm and Precipice and Other Pieces (Selected extracts) – London: Faber & Faber, 1942
The Serpent – London: Faber & Faber, 1943
The Green Isle of the Great Deep – London: Faber & Faber, 1944
The Key of the Chest – London: Faber & Faber, 1945
The Drinking Well – London: Faber & Faber, 1946
The Shadow – London: Faber & Faber, 1948
The Silver Bough – London: Faber & Faber, 1948
The Lost Chart – London: Faber & Faber, 1949
Highland Pack (Essays) – London: Faber & Faber, 1949
The White Hour, and Other Stories (Short stories) – London: Faber & Faber, 1950
The Well at the World's End – London: Faber & Faber, 1951
Bloodhunt – London: Faber & Faber, 1952
The Other Landscape – London: Faber & Faber, 1954
The Atom of Delight (Autobiographical) – London: Faber & Faber, 1956

Posthumous Publications

Landscape and Light – Essays by Neil M. Gunn edited by Alistair McCleery – Aberdeen: Aberdeen University Press, 1987
Neil M. Gunn: Selected Letters edited by J. B. Pick – Edinburgh: Polygon, 1987
The Man Who Came Back, Short Stories and Essays edited by Margery McCulloch – Edinburgh: Polygon, 1991
Poems and related early work collected by C. J. L. Stokoe – Ampthill: Peglet Press, 1994
The Poaching at Grianan – Edinburgh: Merchiston Publishing, 2005
Landscape to Light, Dunbeath: Whittles Publishing, 2009

Major Secondary Literature

Burns, John – *A Celebration of the Light, Zen in the Novels of Neil Gunn*, Edinburgh: Canongate, 1988. Late in his life Neil M. Gunn came across Zen Buddahism an discovered similarities and parallels to his own writing on insight and illumination. John Burns looks at this relationship and highlights the universal themes contained in Gunn's writings.

Gifford, Douglas – *Neil M. Gunn and Lewis Grassic Gibbon*, Edinburgh: Oliver & Boyd, 1983.
A study comparing and contrasting these two major Scottish novelists with a detailed look at Gunn's *The Silver Darlings* and Gibbon's *A Scots Quair*.

Hart, F. R. and J. B. Pick – *Neil M. Gunn: A Highland Life* by London: John Murray, 1981.
The first full, and now, definitive biography of Neil Gunn by two writers who knew him well and write with insight and understanding.

McCulloch, Margery – *The Novels of Neil M. Gunn, A Critical Study*, Edinburgh: Scottish Academic Press, 1987.
A critical study of all Gunn's novels which favours the earlier work and attempts to place the novels in their literary context and explores the relationship between the fiction and non–fiction writing of Neil Gunn.

Morrison, David (Editor) – *Essays on Neil M. Gunn* edited by David Morrison – Thurso: John Humphries, 1971.
Contains four essays on Neil Gunn's novels including work by J. B. Caird and F. R. Hart.

Pick, J. B. – *Neil M. Gunn*, Tavistock: Northcote House Publishers, 2004.
An excellent succinct study of Gunn's life and work by a writer who knew and corresponded with Gunn over a number of years and who writes with perception and insight.

Price, Richard – *The Fabulous Matter of Fact, The Poetics of Neil M. Gunn*, Edinburgh: Edinburgh University Press, 1991.
A comprehensive look at both Gunn's written work and the background and context of his writing from the literary renaissance of the early twentieth century and its influences to its place in European modernism.

Scott, Alexander and Douglas Gifford (Editors) – *Neil M. Gunn, The Man and the Writer* Edinburgh: William Blackwood, 1973.
The first major work devoted to the writing of Neil Gunn. Twenty essays by major writers and critics on subjects from biography to specific novels, styles and bibliography.

Stokoe, by C. J. L. – *A Bibliography of the Works of Neil M. Gunn*, Aberdeen: Aberdeen University Press, 1987.
A detailed and comprehensive bibliography of all Neil Gunn's writings including broadcasts and unpublished material.

Gunn, Dairmid and Isobel Murray (Editors) – *Neil Gunn's Country, Essays in Celebration of Neil Gunn*, Edinburgh: Chambers, 1991.
Range of essays by people who knew Neil Gunn the man covering both his work and his life. Contains biographical and literary assessment.

Neil M. Gunn website

www.neilgunn.org.uk
Contains biographical and bibliographical information, news and resources.